Praise for *A Walk In The Dark*

I have known Don and Eva Piper for close to twenty years, and I am proud to call them friends. We served on the staff at FBC in Pasadena, Texas, for almost ten years together. What a blessing both of them were to me during those years. This book by Eva will be a blessing to everyone who reads it. She knows firsthand how life can quickly take a painful turn and the heartache that accompanies such a nightmare. She also knows how God can see you through the devastating experiences of life and somehow bring you out stronger than you were before. I highly recommend this book to all who want to not only survive the storms of life but to *thrive again* after the winds have stopped blowing!

—Jon Redmond, assistant pastor, First
Baptist Church, Pasadena, Texas

In *A Walk Through the Dark*, Eva Piper reveals what it's like to suddenly become a caregiver to a loved one. Her story is riveting, but it's also filled with practical information on how to provide the support system that is needed when you are living in a new kind of normal. This book is a ⬚⬚⬚⬚⬚⬚⬚ ⬚⬚⬚⬚⬚⬚⬚ ⬚⬚⬚ ngs to grow in faith and provide tan⬚ ⬚⬚⬚⬚⬚ ⬚⬚⬚ ⬚⬚⬚⬚⬚⬚⬚⬚ :ted turn.

rol Kent, speaker and author,
When I Lay My Isaac Down

Eva Piper candidly and compassionately shares her experiences in *A Walk Through the Dark*. The redemption and hope of this book shows us how to walk with the confidence and assurance of The Light. For all of us who have struggled with experiencing the pain and questions that come along with our fragile lives--this is a must read.

—Kathy Troccoli, singer,
songwriter, speaker, author

The extraordinarily important contribution of Eva Piper's , *A Walk Through The Dark*, to the Body of Christ, is its ability to grip your emotions and thoughts, will help you make a decision to serve the One who called us to salvation as we serve the ones in need closest to us. Illuminating insights from a person who has been there and so candidly shares her way to peace and victory.

—BECKY KEENAN, PASTOR,
GULF MEADOWS CHURCH

I laid down Don Piper's book after reading it during a week-long personal retreat at a monastery while trying to process the loss of several family members. My thought was, "I sure would like to meet the wife of the man who spent *90 Minutes in Heaven*". She must have a most fascinating story of her own. Millions of caretakers will find themselves ministered to by Eva's book.

—DAVID BURRIER, CHIEF DEVELOPMENT AND
COMMUNITY RELATIONS OFFICER, HOPE MINISTRIES

A WALK
THROUGH
THE DARK

A WALK
THROUGH
THE DARK

How My Husband's
90 Minutes in Heaven
Deepened My Faith *for a* Lifetime

EVA PIPER

with CECIL MURPHEY

Thomas Nelson
Since 1798

NASHVILLE DALLAS MEXICO CITY RIO DE JANEIRO

Published in Nashville, Tennessee, by Thomas Nelson. Thomas Nelson is a trademark of Thomas Nelson, Inc.

Thomas Nelson, Inc., titles may be purchased in bulk for educational, business, fund-raising, or sales promotional use. For information, please e-mail SpecialMarkets@ThomasNelson.com.

Unless otherwise indicated, Scripture quotations are taken from The Holy Bible, New Living Translation. Copyright © 1996, 2004, 2007 by Tyndale House Foundation. Used by permission of Tyndale House Publishers, Inc., Carol Stream, Illinois, 60188. All rights reserved. Scripture quotations marked NIV are taken from the Holy Bible, New International Version®, NIV®. Copyright © 1973, 1978, 1984 by Biblica, Inc.™ Used by permission of Zondervan. All rights reserved worldwide. www.zondervan.com

Library of Congress Cataloging-in-Publication Data

Piper, Eva, 1952-
    A walk through the dark : how my husband's 90 minutes in heaven deepened my faith for a lifetime / Eva Piper ; with Cecil Murphey.
        p. cm.
    ISBN 978-1-4002-0470-0
    1. Piper, Eva, 1952- 2. Spiritual biography--Texas. 3. Spiritual life--Christianity. 4. Fear--Religious aspects--Christianity. 5. Spouses--Death--Psychological aspects. 6. Piper, Don, 1950- I. Title.
    BR1725.P543A3 2013
    231.7'3'092--dc23
    [B]

                                2013000162

Printed in the United States of America

13 14 15 16 17 RRD 6 5 4 3 2 1

In loving memory of my mom, Ethel Pentecost.

She was a model of strength, will, and utter determination.

God, Family, Country

Contents

FOREWORD

Recently, I fell down the stairs of our home. Because falling down has become somewhat of a habit for me, my friend Cliff McArdle has observed that I've "fallen in some of the nicest places in town."

I've discovered that falling down seems to go with being in a horrific car wreck, badly breaking both of my legs, and having many surgeries on those legs. Eva was there for those operations and she's been there after each fall, including the most recent one.

As I completed my latest fall to the bottom of our stairwell, I was reminded of the helpless feeling on the way down. I had no control over my body; there was absolutely nothing I could do to stop the tumbling. Gravity ruled the moment.

That's similar to the situation in which I found myself on the morning of January 18, 1989, when a big truck struck me head-on and killed me. I had no control over my death or my life. I couldn't have possibly grasped that day the extent to which others would control my life in the days to come.

It took the combined efforts of some of the finest medical professionals on the planet, thousands of prayer warriors, hundreds of church members, devoted family members, and dear friends to put this humpty dumpty back together again. However, the utter faithfulness of one woman was the most crucial to my recovery.

She is my wife of nearly forty years, Eva Pentecost Piper.

Three weeks before the accident, we had celebrated our fifteenth anniversary. In the following two years, a virtual lifetime of hard decisions and deep emotions befell us. The course of our lives changed. We still have the scars to show for our trials. Most of mine are visible; hers, not so much.

Eva had given birth to our three children, Nicole, Chris, and Joe. From the moment we brought them home from the hospital we nurtured, cherished, and guided them. As we parented our children, I'm certain that Eva never contemplated having to care for an utterly helpless thirty-eight-year-old husband at the same time. She was a thirty-six-year-old daughter, the eldest of a retired Air Force chief master sergeant from Missouri, an elementary school teacher, a gifted pianist, and a devoted Christian mother and wife.

In some ways, nothing prepared her for the shocking news of my terrible accident. But as you will learn, in other ways, she had been prepared for my horrific accident.

I believe that because of her triumph over this ordeal in our lives you will be inspired to overcome too. You can learn from her successes and challenges. You can laugh at our foibles, weep at our most vulnerable moments, and cheer her enormous victories. In the end, you'll be better prepared to conquer disaster and defeat helplessness and hopelessness.

Hundreds of thousands of people have heard me say in books I've written, media appearances, and in person, "Eva is the hero of my story. I survived the accident. She overcame it."

In *A Walk in the Dark*, you'll find out how she did it. Eva, along with God and a cast of thousands, did it.

That morning, January 18, 1989, two ordinary people were doing what they had been called to do. I was on my way to the church where God had called me to serve. Eva was teaching her students at school, a calling that I believe is one of God's most important and demanding.

In an instant, our lives were irrevocably and dramatically changed. My body lay dreadfully mangled amid twisted metal and shattered glass. She stood across the desk from her school principal as she heard the words, "I'm afraid I have some bad news for you."

A few yeas ago, if you had told me that I'd be writing a foreword for her book about overcoming crisis and heartbreak, I'd have scoffed at the suggestion. I have certainly demonstrated that I don't have the gift of prophecy. Otherwise I might have anticipated the remarkable response to our mighty challenge. I saw none of this coming, including this book from the hero of the story—Eva.

When you start to "fall down the stairs," there is that moment when you realize that you have no control over what's going on. You simply experience the plunge and see where it takes you. At least in the case of my lovely bride, Eva Piper, I'm delighted that it has taken her here, to this book. I believe that it will be treasured for generations as a textbook for overcoming, from someone who did overcome.

Eva, I honor your determination in the face of staggering odds, your unwavering faithfulness in the darkest of nights, and your steadfast love, even to someone who was mostly unlovable, me.

Eva, you are the hero of our story.

Don Piper
August 2012

1.

THE DARKNESS BEGINS

On January 18, 1989, my husband died. In a matter of seconds, I went from living in the light to walking in the dark.

And I've always been afraid of the dark.

I can give no compelling reason for my fear, but it's there. As a child, I went to sleep with a night-light. At night I still keep the bathroom light on and leave the door slightly open. When I enter our home, I hit the light switches; the more the better. No one will ever find me walking through a pitch-black field or along an unlit beach.

It's not just the physical darkness. I also strongly dislike being "kept in the dark." I'm one of those people who reads the first chapter of a book to get the plot and then immediately skips over to the final chapter. Something in me has to know how everything turns out. Only then can I enjoy the middle of the book.

On that day in 1989, I began a walk having no idea how or where it would end, or how long it would take. I couldn't have prepared for the darkness that began on that chilly, damp January afternoon.

Looking back, I sometimes wonder why I had no hint that anything terrible would happen. Even now, I'll convince myself that I've fully embraced the light; and, without warning, I'm stumbling in the darkness again.

That Wednesday, January 18, started like any other normal day for me. I was teaching first grade at Stevenson Primary School in Alvin, Texas. Less than two years earlier, we had moved from Bossier City, Louisiana, to Alvin after Don, my husband, accepted the position of youth minister at South Park Baptist Church.

Monday morning, Don left to make the hour-and-a-half drive in his Ford Escort to Trinity Pines, a Baptist retreat center north of Houston. The center was presenting a three-day conference focusing on church planting (how to start new churches). Don's big dream was to start his own congregation. He had been enthusiastic about the opportunity to learn more about how to get a church started.

Don had mentioned the conference to me several weeks earlier. I had sensed his excitement about the event and encouraged him to attend. "They invited spouses to come along," Don had told me. "Do you want to go with me?"

"Yes!"

I've tried to support Don throughout his ministry and felt that going with him would help me understand some of the issues he would face in establishing a new church. I decided to take three personal days and accompany him.

I didn't get to attend many events with Don, so I eagerly looked forward to spending time with him, as well as learning more about evangelistic outreach in communities. Selfishly, I was looking forward to having some "away time" with my husband.

Even though there would be several hundred ministers present, I thought how nice it would be not to have one of our kids clamoring for our attention. Since moving to Texas, Don and I had had very little couple time to talk and enjoy each other's presence. In Bossier City, my parents had lived around the corner, so getting a babysitter wasn't a problem. We didn't have that luxury in Texas.

Seeing that the children were provided for didn't prove to be a big problem. Nicole was in seventh grade, and her best friend was Kim Chisolm. Nicole already spent a lot of her free time with the Chisolm family; they assured me it wouldn't be an imposition for our daughter to stay there.

Our twin sons, Chris and Joe, were in the second grade. Another family at South Park Church offered to keep the boys while we were gone.

I had gotten the time off, we'd made arrangements for our children, and everything was set for us to leave Monday morning for Trinity Pines. We'd stay for lunch before starting back. That would give us a relaxing drive home to Alvin, with plenty of time to arrive for Wednesday night services.

But as it turned out, I didn't go.

Less than a week before the conference, a number of new students entered the school. Several of them ended up in my first-grade class.

After trying to figure out how to get the new children assimilated into the class and into the school system and still go with Don, I realized I couldn't get everything done before we left. It wouldn't have been fair to my substitute to deal with the new children along with the other issues a substitute encounters.

"I don't know their reading level," I told Don. "I can't leave them until I've tested them and know how they fit into class. I can't go with you." I was disappointed that I had to drop out. It would have been an excellent conference for both of us.

Don was also disappointed, but he understood.

———

Monday at school was normal for me—or as normal as a classroom can be with six new students, all first-graders, who transferred into the school in the middle of the year. It took a little more time and effort to get the six children tested, but by the end of the school day on Monday, I had accomplished that.

Tuesday went well. Wednesday morning was uneventful; so were lunch and recess. On Wednesday evenings, all five of our family members usually met at the church for the regular midweek evening events. We ate dinner at the church and then attended our individual activities.

Nicole was involved with Acteens, a mission organization for teenage girls. The boys were members of Royal Ambassadors (RAs), a mission group for boys in grades one through six. I was a choir member, and we practiced on Wednesday evenings. Don had planned to teach at what we called our midweek prayer service. So all five of us were involved. I expected Don to meet us at the church, and we planned to drive home in two cars.

Nothing unusual. Just our regular Wednesday arrangement. But that night we didn't meet at the church. In fact, it would be many Wednesdays before the five of us were together again at church.

———

The weather that Wednesday in Alvin was chilly and damp. At times heavy rain hit and then turned into drizzle. Either way, it was miserable. My classroom at school was located at the end of the hall, so I could hear the downpour beat on the metal covering over the sidewalks that led to the temporary buildings. As I peered out the glass doors that led outside, the world looked cold, damp, and dismal.

Then came my personal darkness. At about one thirty it began to descend.

I was teaching in my classroom about ninety minutes before the end of my day. I sat at one of the kidney-shaped tables, working with one of the four reading groups. The other students were at work at their desks. We had turned the classroom into a winter wonderland, and occasionally I would pause, gaze around the room, and enjoy looking at what we had done. We don't often have snow in South Texas, so it was a tradition to decorate the rooms with a winter theme to help the students understand what winter looks like in the North.

Students had made snowflakes that hung from ceiling tiles. There were also winter pictures made with Ivory detergent snow "paint" and snowmen made of cotton balls.

One bulletin board still held the New Year's resolutions written by the students after they returned from the Christmas holidays. Except for the small group with me, the children sat in the traditional brown desks with chairs. The beige-painted, cinder-block room didn't have any windows except a small vertical one on the door.

A slight noise attracted my attention. I looked up from the book I held as the classroom door opened about three inches. Glenda Sosa, a tall, redheaded instructional aide, motioned for me.

I shook my head and pointed to the children as if to say, "I can't stop now. I'm in the middle of a lesson."

Glenda motioned again, and the intense look on her face said, "Come anyway. It's important."

I nodded, but it seemed strange. Ordinarily, she would have said something at the door or motioned to let me know what she wanted. Not this time.

I held up my hand to say, "Give me a few seconds," then turned to the children. "I'll be right back. I want you to be quiet at your desks while Mrs. Piper speaks to someone at the door."

I put the book down and walked toward her.

"They need you in the office right away," Glenda said in a voice that didn't sound quite normal, "I'll watch your class for you."

I thanked her and left.

The first thing that went through my head was a question: *Have I aggravated a parent?* That's one of the realities of teaching. During my career I had encountered a few students who didn't like something I did or said and told their parents, who complained to the principal. There had been occasions when I'd sat patiently in a parent-teacher conference, listening to what a fellow teacher called "a complaint that you're infringing on their little darling's rights." By working together we usually came to an understanding, and the year would continue with no further problems. As I walked toward the office, I couldn't think of anyone who might have complained recently.

A second thought hit me: *Maybe I didn't turn in an important form, or I forgot something I was supposed to have done.* I was still new to the district and learning the ins and outs of what was expected.

My third thought was about our twin sons. Even though we kept them in separate classes, they still found ways to get in trouble. There were never serious difficulties—they were good boys—but being in separate classrooms didn't mean they couldn't find ways to be together. The restroom, the cafeteria, and the playground were twin-friendly areas and places for them to conceive of ways to have fun.

Chris had always been outgoing, while Joe was quiet and reserved—at least until he got to know people. Together they could dream up all kinds of mischief (and often did), both at home and at school. I thought of a time earlier in the year when I had been accompanying one of my students to the office. Around the corner came Chris with his second-grade teacher, and around the other corner I spotted Joe with his teacher. I took my student by the hand, turned, and went back to my classroom. I said softly to myself, "I don't want to know about this." (I never did learn what happened.)

The boys. It has to be the twins. I wonder what they've done now.

I walked into the office, and as soon as the assistant principal, Mary Nell Douglas, saw me, she got up from her desk, rushed over, wrapped her arms around me, and gave me a hug. A tall woman, who exemplified a professional manner in character and dress, Mary Nell was her typical warm, caring, and friendly self.

Even though it was my first year at Stevenson, Mary Nell had made me feel welcome and a part of the family. I especially appreciated that she offered advice in a positive manner. She was popular with the staff because we felt she had our best interests at heart.

Just one thing was off: an embrace wasn't her usual method of greeting me. Before I could speak, she said, "We've gotten a call from your church."

"What—"

"Don's been in a wreck. We're trying to find out what happened."

I stared at her, taking in what she had said.

In that moment, God spoke to me. I didn't hear an audible voice, yet the message was so clear I couldn't doubt the reality. *This will be difficult, but it's going to be okay. Don has two broken legs and a broken arm.*

To some, that probably sounds strange, especially because it was so specific. God had spoken, and there were no doubts. I believe God whispered to me to give me the perfect peace of which the Bible speaks and to prepare me for what was ahead.

"It was a car accident," Mary Nell added. "I don't know where."

I didn't know where Don was, what had happened, or how seriously he was hurt, but a deep, inner calm came over me.

As I stared at her, I could see she was troubled, and I could sense her concern for me. "It's all right," I said. "It's going to be all right."

I took a deep breath to steady my voice and to keep from crying. At heart I'm an emotional person, easily brought to tears; however, I've discovered that I can sometimes control those tears. It's a trick I learned back in high school when I started wearing contacts. Crying made my mascara run, getting into my eyes and wreaking havoc with my contacts. Over the years I'd become an expert at controlling my tears in public, but this time, even after God's assuring words, drops of salty liquid slipped down my face while I tried to wipe them away.

"Who called?" I asked. "What do you know? Where is he?"

"I don't know anything more. Not yet."

I sat down in the big leather chair in front of Mary Nell's desk and put my head in my hands.

———

Parts of the next half hour remain blurred in my mind. Two of my best friends from church rushed to the school. Suzan Mauldin taught at Alvin High School and left her classes to be with me. Susan Long was a nurse on duty, but she was able to leave her job so she could come too.

Both were of medium height and slender. Suzan Mauldin had shoulder-length, dark hair, which she often wore in a ponytail. She was always tastefully and stylishly dressed. Her students loved her because she was accessible and easy to talk to.

Susan Long was the athletic type, blonde, and blue-eyed. Her typical outfit was a pair of jeans and a T-shirt. My son Chris says he remembers her having kind eyes. I guess that characteristic goes along with being a nurse.

Both women had reached out to me after we moved to Alvin. Like them, I was a young, working mother, and we connected. The Long and Mauldin families were active in the youth group, as well as teaching Sunday school, going on retreats, and serving as counselors at youth camps. Suzan and Susan had taken it on themselves (which was typical of them) to look after the newcomer—me.

I wasn't surprised to see them in Mary Nell's office. It's what friends do; they show up for each other.

Mark Evans, the minister of music from South Park, arrived at about the same time. Soon there were others—a small office full of people—all there to express their sympathy and concern. I vaguely wondered why so many had come.

It's not as if Don has died, I thought as I looked around. I already knew about the broken arm and broken legs before we had any report, so I was calmer than my comforters.

Still, I was surprised at the number of people who came. After all, we had only been in Alvin a short time. It encouraged me to know that so many individuals cared. Because Don and I were away from our own families for the first time in our married life, my new friends' presence touched my heart. The fact that they had made the effort and taken the time to come made me aware of their kindness and their affection.

As I greeted each one, I thought of something my mother often said while I was growing up: "Actions speak louder than words." I appreciated them even more because I knew that those who came weren't there out of duty. That was obvious. They came because they cared. I hugged them as they entered and tried to thank them for coming. I write *tried* because sometimes tears flowed and words wouldn't come. But I realized that words weren't needed, so I didn't feel embarrassed when I couldn't articulate my feelings.

Before long, more church members arrived and filled the office. In all, probably fifteen to twenty individuals showed up.

Most of them didn't stay, but their coming meant so much. They walked into the office, hugged me, said a few kind words, and left. Others, like Susan, Suzan, and Mark, stayed the entire time. Some were teachers from the school across town where I had taught the year before, but several were church members, along with a few school administrators.

I still knew nothing—only what God had whispered to me. I didn't tell anyone about that message, but I tried to assure them I was fine. After several minutes I became aware that I was comforting them because they seemed more upset than I was.

While we waited for further information, I slowly surveyed the room and stared at my friends who had gathered. They probably said many things, but their words were lost to me almost as soon as they were spoken. However, they did one thing that was important and something I'll never forget: each one of them wrapped his or her arms around me and held me. From every person, it felt like a spontaneous gesture, which made it even more powerful. In the years since, I've learned that an embrace can often speak more, comfort more, and convey more love than the wisest or most profound words.

Mary Nell kept dialing number after number, trying to find out something, anything. Following up every lead she could, she was determined to obtain more information.

Susan grabbed an extra telephone directory and went into another office to use the phone. She called every area hospital to ask if a patient named Don Piper had been brought in.

At each hospital, the operator replied, "We have no patient by that name."

The ringing of the phone in the outer office interrupted the stillness in the room. Seconds later, the secretary transferred the call to Mary Nell's office.

She listened a few seconds before she announced to all of us, "It's the hospital in Huntsville." (Huntsville was about 130 miles away.) Someone was apparently giving her basic information, and she put her hand over the phone and said, "Don has been taken to Huntsville Memorial Hospital, just off I-45."

She listened again before she held the phone out to me. "Do you want to speak to Don?"

I could see the relief on her face. Her expression seemed to say, *See, it's not so bad.*

Of course I wanted to speak to him. I took the phone and said hello.

"We have Mr. Piper," a woman replied, identifying herself as a nurse. "Would Mrs. Piper like to speak with him?"

"Yes, I would. I'm Mrs. Piper."

"He is unable to hold the phone himself, so I'm going to put it up to his ear."

"Don! Don! How are—"

"I just wanted to come home . . . I just wanted to come home." After that he groaned and I couldn't understand anything else.

I will never forget that groaning because it was such a horrible sound, especially coming from someone I know is strong. Tears filled my eyes again, and I didn't know what more to say.

Susan took the phone from me and spoke with the nurse. In retrospect, I have to say I was in shock. I don't remember if I continued crying, but I probably did. I'm prone to tears when I get emotional, but it's not my nature to scream or shriek.

As soon as she hung up, Susan said in a very even and professional voice, "They are doing some assessment."

"What does that mean?" I think I asked, or perhaps I only wanted to.

"He's at the Huntsville hospital. They're going to assess his injuries and stabilize him before they transport him to Hermann Memorial Hospital." Hermann Memorial is one of the anchor hospitals of the world-renowned Texas Medical Center.*

In fact, it's the hospital I was born in while my dad was stationed at Ellington Air Force Base. "This much the nurse told me. Don has two broken legs and a broken arm."

I knew that. I hadn't told anyone that God had spoken, but the message from Susan brought immediate peace.

Everything was going to be all right. If God had been right about Don's injuries, then he must be right about everything turning out okay. Little did I know what it would take to get to that point.

---

* The terms *Hermann Hospital* and *Texas Medical Center* are used interchangeably throughout this story.

2.

GETTING READY

S usan's report that the medical staff had to assess Don's injuries before moving him to Hermann Memorial Hospital made sense. It also explained to me his groaning on the phone. It made better sense when I realized they had probably withheld medication until they knew how badly he was hurt.

They were going to move him, so that was encouraging. *They wouldn't move him if he were badly injured.* I didn't know if that was correct, but that idea helped keep my spirits up.

Later, as I thought back through everything, I was convinced God gave me the concrete fact regarding the broken bones before we heard any reports, because as awful as they are, I could understand broken bones.

While we waited for more information, my mind kept returning to two things: Don was alive, and I had spoken to him on the phone.

He is going to be all right.

Even though the message through Susan was accurate, no one had given me any idea of how badly Don had been hurt. Later, after I learned the extent of his injuries, I would have to fall back on those special words from the Lord: *This will be difficult, but it's going to be okay.*

In the days ahead, my faith floundered at times, and I questioned God. Those were the worst moments. Most of the time, however, I was able to remind myself that God had spoken words of comfort to assure me that I didn't need to worry about my husband.

———

After a group embrace and phone call from Huntsville, all of us stood around awkwardly, as if no one was sure what to do next. I glanced at my watch and realized that I had been out of the classroom for nearly thirty minutes.

"I have to get back to my children," I said.

My friends were concerned for me, and most of them thought it wasn't a good idea for me to go back into the classroom.

I shook my head. "Joe reminded me again this morning that he and other second graders are coming to my room to present a play for us. I need to be there."

That was an important event to me. For Joe, being in a play was a big deal because he's typically not outgoing. That was a huge step for him. He had been excited and, quiet as he is, he had talked about the play several times. I couldn't disappoint him. Besides, I didn't want him to come to my classroom and ask, "Where's my mom?" I had to be there for him.

"I have to go back to my classroom," I said again—firmly—to my friends. I assured them that I was all right and that everything was in God's hands. As I encouraged them, I also assured them that I was at peace. Those weren't empty words, because I believed exactly what I said. I didn't realize it then, but it would be only one of many times I would find myself trying to comfort others who had come to encourage me.

"You're sure you're all right?" I heard that question at least three times. Each time I said I was fine.

And I was.

At least I was then.

Four or five of my friends stayed in the office, waiting for further word; others went back to work.

"Wait a minute," Mark said to me. "After school I'll follow your car to your house so you can pick up what you need. Then I'll drive you to the hospital."

I don't know if I thanked him then, but his offer sounded like such a gift to me. I could have driven myself, but I was glad I didn't have to do that.

"You don't have to—"

"I'll be here to pick you up," he said. "And don't worry about the evening service. We already have that covered." Don was supposed to have preached, and I was grateful they had handled it without talking to me.

Like almost everyone in the area, I knew about the Houston Medical Center. As a pastor, Don had made multiple hospital visits there. I recalled him saying what a nightmare it was to get around in the area and find the right parking garage for the right hospital. Fifteen hospitals are connected to the medical complex.

It was a relief to know I wasn't going to have to make that drive and go through the pressure of finding a place to park.

One of my fears of the "dark" that continues even today is the fear of getting lost. I have a good sense of direction but feel more comfortable when I know exactly where I'm headed. That was in the days before GPS or Google Maps. While I've always felt comfortable driving in the city, parking garages make me nervous, especially when I don't know where to enter. Just the mention of the Medical Center usually brought horror stories of people getting lost both coming and going.

"Thank you," I said to Mark. "I'll meet you in the parking lot after school."

"I'll take Chris and Joe home with me," Susan said. "So you don't need to worry about the boys."

Suzan Mauldin had to hurry back to the high school before classes dismissed. Before she left she insisted that she wanted to help and to be there for me. "Keep me informed."

I promised I would, and she hugged me before she left.

I knew Nicole would be going home with Kim Chisolm because that was the usual Wednesday routine. I asked someone to call Kim's mom to let her know what was happening. That way she could keep an eye on Nicole until I could talk to her myself. I didn't think Nicole had heard about her dad, but Alvin is a small town, and news travels fast. I didn't want her to overhear a conversation before I had the opportunity to reassure her that everything was going to be fine.

With my kids cared for and the assurance that the medical staff were doing everything they could for Don, I felt life was moving back toward normal—at least our normal Wednesday. I was sure we'd learn to adjust after Don got home.

God's peace truly filled my heart. I was able to compartmentalize my emotions so that I didn't worry. I could do that because I knew Don was in God's hands.

I hurried back to my classroom so I'd be ready for the second graders' presentation. When I opened the door, Joe's class was already inside the room, standing in front, waiting for me so they could begin. He smiled, and I knew I had done the right thing by insisting on returning to the room.

Joe and his classmates presented their little play. I can't remember anything about it, although I'm usually able to recall things like that. Despite the peace of God then and my ability to take it in, later events caused many things to blur in my mind.

Or perhaps I faked my cheeriness as well as my absorption in the play. I don't know; maybe I was numb, but I truly felt at peace. Afterward, I vaguely remember finishing out the school day and preparing my first graders for dismissal.

Teachers have to stay after the children leave, and on most days, Joe and Chris would come to my classroom to wait until it was time to go home. I wanted to talk with them and explain what had happened before Susan picked them up. I knew that was going to be difficult. As the time passed, I was having a harder time holding it together, so I arranged for someone to bring them to the classroom of my friend Barbara Buckley. She had been Chris's first grade teacher, and they had formed a special bond. Barbara had also become my close friend as well as a colleague. I decided that if she was in the room with me, I would have a backup, someone to jump in if I wasn't able to explain to the boys what was happening. I was waiting in Barbara's classroom when the boys walked in. They were both wearing jeans and long-sleeved shirts and carrying their backpacks.

Joe was still excited about the play. Chris, as usual, had questions in his eyes. Something was up, and he knew it.

I knelt and wrapped my arms around both of them. "I need to tell you something," I said.

Both boys stared at me, worried looks on their faces, and neither said anything. They could tell I had been crying, but I tried to be as strong as possible for their sake. Having Barbara in the room helped me focus on talking to the boys without giving in to my emotions.

"Your daddy has been in a car wreck," I explained. I continued by saying that I didn't know any details, but I mentioned the broken bones. "That's all we know right now." I gave each a hug and told them I loved them.

Both of them said, "I love you too, Mom."

Their little faces showed they were trying to understand what was happening. They were old enough to know about car wrecks but still young enough not to grasp the possible seriousness. It took all I had to continue in as calm a voice as I could manage.

"You'll have to stay with Mrs. Buckley until Susan Long can get here. She'll pick you up and take you with her to church tonight."

They both nodded, their eyes big and round.

"Mark Evans is driving me to the hospital to see your daddy. I probably won't be back before bedtime, and that's why Susan is taking you to her house." I felt as if I were speaking like a robot. I didn't want to frighten the boys, so I said as little as possible.

To their credit, they didn't protest. They may have asked questions, but if they did, my mind has blotted that out of my memory.

As I spoke to the boys, inside my head I pictured two cars colliding. Don had always been an extremely careful driver, so I assumed someone had run a red light, crossed the center stripe, or struck him from behind and knocked his car against an embankment.

It's not going to be too terribly awful.

When my mind started to get too heavily into what might have happened, I reminded myself that two broken legs and a broken arm aren't life threatening. Terrible. Painful. But our limbs mend. I could see him with a cast on both legs and his arm. Don had always been so active that he wouldn't like that, but a couple of months and he'd be normal again.

Yes, we could cope.

3.

STEPPING INTO THE UNKNOWN

After I was sure the boys were all right, I grabbed my purse and stuffed my canvas bag with school papers, my grade book, and a calculator. The nine-week reporting period would end soon, so I needed to get tests corrected and grades entered into the grade book. In those days, teachers still averaged their own grades and filled in grade sheets for report cards.

As I tried to rush out of the building to meet Mark in the parking lot, Mary Nell stopped me and offered to drive me home. "You shouldn't be driving," she said.

"I'll be all right," I said. "I really will." It touched me that she was concerned I might be too upset to drive from Alvin to our home in Friendswood about ten miles away. I assured her and the other staff members who were still there that I could handle the trip. "Besides, Mark will be driving right behind me."

It wouldn't have occurred to me to break down in front of them, no matter how shaky I felt. In our family while I was growing up, we didn't allow emotions to get in the way of doing what had to be done. Right then, I needed to get home, and that's what I was going to do. I pushed everything out of my consciousness and focused on what I had to do immediately.

I got into my light-blue Ford Tempo. I tried to relax as I drove the ten miles to our house and in my mind checked off the things I would need to do. The most important was changing clothes; I didn't want to wear the same outfit I had worn all day at school. As soon as I parked, I waved at Mark and hurried inside.

I changed into a pair of blue sweats and a white shirt. I tend to get cold in places like hospitals, so I picked out a jacket as well. Before I left I paused to think if there was anything else I might need if I spent the night. I grabbed my glasses then my contact lens container and shoved them into my purse along with a comb and toothbrush.

I was almost at the door when I thought of something else. The previous semester our music teacher's husband had had a massive heart attack while he was in West Texas. They'd transported him to the hospital, and his wife had hurried out there to be with him. I remember her saying that the hardest thing for her was coming up with change for the pay phones. That was in the days before cell phones and the Internet.

She had made a point of describing the bank of phones against one wall. "I never seemed to have enough coins," she'd said, "and every day I had to hunt around, asking for change."

A month before the accident, the youth of South Park Baptist Church gave Don and me what they call a money tree. Adults pinned dollars on the tree (actually a small tree branch), but the kids, who didn't have a lot of money, gave us silver. The money tree sat in a painted flowerpot, and the teenagers filled the pot with enough coins to hold up the tree. I'd thrown away the "tree" but left the change in the flowerpot.

As I headed toward the door, I picked up the container, dumped the coins into a brown lunch bag, and put it inside my purse.

For me to think about the pay phones is one of those small but important things. Although I had no awareness of God speaking to me, I believe the Lord led me to stuff the money into the paper sack. Those coins were exactly what I needed in the days ahead. So many times I would need to call someone, just to talk or to hear a kind voice. I'm thankful I didn't have to worry about the frustration my teacher-friend had encountered. Our God watches out for even the smallest detail.

———

Mark drove me to the Chisolms' house so I could see Nicole. I wanted to be the one to tell her what little I knew. As the oldest, and truly a daddy's girl, it was essential that she be told in person.

The Chisolms lived out in the country, and their house was the perfect Texas rural home, complete with shutters and a front-yard fence. Nicole was looking out the front window when we drove up.

At first she probably thought nothing of it because we were in Mark's car, but after she saw me, she raced outside to meet me. The expression on her face made me realize she sensed something wasn't right.

"What's wrong?" she asked. Nicole is a beautiful girl with bright, green eyes. She has always been tall for her age, and at that time she was in the seventh grade and had curly brown hair (courtesy of a permanent). Nicole has a bubbly personality and wins friends easily. She also takes seriously the role of being the eldest.

She and I have always been close, so she could read my face better than the boys could.

"You've been crying, haven't you?"

Instead of answering, I said, "I need to talk to you about something."

I draped my arm over her shoulder, and we walked inside and sat down. In a calm voice I told her that her father had been in an accident, which was about the same thing I had told the boys. Again, I deliberately tried to be as positive as I could so I didn't frighten her. Though she was only twelve, she felt like a mother figure to her twin brothers and, at times, acted older than she was. After the boys were born, she often called them "my babies."

She listened quietly. As soon as I paused, she asked, "Is Daddy going to be okay?"

"Yes, he's going to be okay."

"Is the car okay?"

I laughed, but I understood. Nicole was nearly thirteen, and at that age a car is a big deal. "I don't know about the Ford," I said. "I'll have to see about the damage."

She handled the information well, although I could perceive the same questions I had seen in her brothers' eyes earlier, so I said, "Go to church tonight with Kim. You can spend the night with her. After that we'll figure out how things will work." I added, "Everything is going to be fine. God is with us."

"I love you, Mom. Tell Daddy I love him." She hugged me good-bye.

Because she was older I had expected more questions, but she took the news quite well. I think she realized how anxious I was to get to the hospital and didn't want to delay me. My guess is she wanted to go with me but understood that wasn't a practical idea.

———

Although it wasn't quite four o'clock when Mark and I headed toward the hospital, the weather was still drizzly, hazy, and darker than normal for that time of day. Later I learned that the examining doctor at Huntsville had wanted to helicopter Don to Houston, but the weather was too bad. Instead, a new ambulance from Huntsville was making its first run to transport him to Houston.

I still had no idea where or how the accident had taken place. Those weren't the kind of questions to which I needed answers right then. I was more concerned about Don's condition than I was about the cause.

As Mark and I drove from my home to Highway 288 and on to the medical center, we had little conversation. I spent most of the trip staring out the passenger-side window.

In many ways I still couldn't comprehend what was happening. It all seemed dreamlike. I would try to think of something, but the thought would fly out of my head before I had a chance to grab it and make it real. The truth is, the weather was a reflection of my state of mind—foggy and misty.

Mark may have tried to say comforting words, but I don't recall. Or perhaps, being sensitive to my need to sit and process, he said nothing most of the time. I seem to remember either his humming a hymn or listening to the local Christian radio station, KSBJ. That would make sense, as we both were actively involved in the music program at the church.

My thoughts flitted from Don's broken bones to the children and back to Don. Image after image came to me, and I tried to absorb everything in the quietness of the car. One thing haunted me—my husband's groaning. No matter how hard I tried to push away that sound, it kept coming back.

At some point it became clear that Mark had something he needed to tell me. He made a slight coughing sound, cleared his throat, and started speaking in a soft voice. It was the type of voice an adult uses when trying to talk to an upset child. Quiet, measured, even. His eyes never left the road as he explained that the church had called with additional information.

"From what we've heard, Don's car was wrecked by an eighteen-wheeler, but we don't know any further details."

That statement shattered my foggy thoughts. *Wreck* meant one thing and implied significant but not necessarily life-threatening results. *But hit by a semi?*

I had seen enough collisions to know that most of the time, crashes with eighteen-wheelers didn't turn out well. An experience during my teenage years had left me with a deep fear of trucks. When one approached me on the freeway, I usually held my breath until either the truck passed me or I'd speeded up so we were no longer side by side.

I'm not sure I responded to Mark. He was probably trying to be kind and not throw everything at me that he knew. I continued to stare out the window, unable to talk. After hearing about the truck, I temporarily lost my sense of peace and was aware of my shallow breathing.

I have to get there. I have to see Don myself . . . How bad is he? I need to get to the hospital.

As illogical as it sounds, I felt that once I arrived at the hospital and was able to be next to Don, things would be better. I wanted answers, and I was sure that whatever was wrong, the doctors could fix it. I also reminded myself that the Hermann Medical Center is world-class, and the top doctors in the country practice there.

Don is going to be fine. The doctors will take care of him . . . Surely, surely they can fix whatever is wrong.

———

We finally arrived at the medical center. It wasn't an unusually long trip, but it seemed that way. Mark had no trouble finding a place to park, so we got out of the car and hurried inside. We followed the signs to the emergency room and approached the admitting desk.

I stated my name and asked if my husband, Donald Piper, had arrived.

"He's in transit," the woman at the desk said. "He should be here soon."

Before I had a chance to ask any more questions, she thrust several sheets of paper at me. "We need you to fill out these insurance forms."

I took the forms from her and stared at them. I had no idea how to fill out those papers. I was thirty-six years old, educated, and an experienced public school teacher, but my husband had always taken care of legal documents and insurance forms. That was a mutual agreement, because I didn't like making big decisions.

A few times I had said to Don, "I don't know where the money is going." He explained everything I asked about, but I honestly didn't really pay attention.

One time he pointed to a drawer where he kept files. "Everything's right in there. You can look at them any time you want."

The truth is, I didn't want to see those files. It was easier to lean on Don and allow him to make the decisions. I felt I had my hands full taking care of our home, our children, and my job. Why did I need to know the boring stuff?

That had been our arrangement since our marriage in 1973. I knew Don's social security number and birth date but not much else. At the time of the accident I didn't even know the name of our insurer, only that they covered the Alvin Independent School District. I didn't know the type of insurance coverage we had or the amount of our deductible. I didn't even carry an insurance card with me.

The experience frightened me. Just being in the emergency wing meant I had stepped into the unknown. As small a matter as it may seem, filling out forms overwhelmed me with anxiety. I liked to know the *answers*, but as I stared at the *questions*, I didn't know what to write.

I handed back the almost-blank forms. "I don't know the answers to all of those things." I gave what information I knew and explained to the receptionist that I'd find out the rest and let the hospital know the next day. She nodded, and I realized that she dealt with such situations every day.

My old life was coming apart, and I felt alone and confused. I had taken one more step on the dark path that I would follow for a long, long time.

4.

FACING THE REALITY

If anyone had asked, I would have said I was calm and aware of everything around me that day in ER. Perhaps I was; or maybe I only thought so at the time.

As I've tried to write about those experiences, I've realized that the passage of time has made various memories erode. Probably more significant, however, is that stress and shock have played even larger roles in dimming parts of those painful experiences. At the time everything was so real that I was convinced I'd never forget a single detail; but as time went on and hundreds of other things happened, the memories faded. Others I've talked to who have gone through traumatic experiences say the same thing.

Instead of complaining, I am comforted to think of it as God putting blinders on some of our more painful memories to shield us from the shock and the pain.

Back in the emergency ward, the woman who had taken the almost blank insurance forms from me pointed to the waiting room and told me to go in there. "He's in transit," she said again.

I remember little about the room except that there were no chairs, only benches. A TV was on, but the volume had been turned too low to hear. Perhaps eight or ten people were already sitting in the large room. Every few minutes a doctor would call for a family, and then they'd leave. Others came in, so there was a lot of movement. Despite all the people, it was quiet—almost as if everyone were afraid to talk too loud.

Mark sat next to me and said nothing, for which I was grateful. I felt lost in my own thoughts, vacillating from peace to anxiety and back to calmness. I prayed for Don when I could focus my mind.

I looked up as two deacons from the South Park Church came toward me. They may have been there before I arrived, but I'm not sure. I can't remember them clearly—not even their names—only that they were there. My head swam as they asked questions.

"Where did this happen?"

"What kind of answers do you have about his condition?"

"How long is he going to be in the hospital?"

I didn't know, and I told them. I appreciated their coming to be with me, but I felt frustrated by not having answers to their questions. I wanted to stay calm, think positively, and pray silently for my husband.

They stayed to support me, but I wasn't able to pay much attention to them. In the back of my mind, I could hear them talking, but I focused on the door. From where I sat, I wouldn't be able to see them bring Don into the hospital, but I assumed someone would come immediately to tell me.

The door to the emergency entrance had one small window, and if I walked over to it, I could peek out and watch ambulances pull up. I couldn't stay there and block the door, but every few minutes I'd get up, walk over, and look outside, hoping Don's ambulance would pull up.

We arrived at the hospital about 4:40 that afternoon. I tried not to keep checking the time or stare at the standard black-and-white clock on the wall. The longer I waited, the more nervous I felt. I finally got up and paced back and forth to give myself something to do.

The pacing didn't help, so after about twenty minutes, I walked over to the nurses' station. "Where are they now?" I asked.

"They're still in transit."

It was the same answer, and I knew the woman didn't have any further information for me, but I couldn't fully relax. For the next hour or so I continued to ask the question repeatedly, and always I received the same calm, neutral response.

No one seemed to know anything, and my level of concern and worry was growing as the large clock ticked off minutes.

About 6:15, I stared through the small, glass partition and saw an ambulance pull up. Bay doors swung open. I'm not sure how, but I knew it had to be Don they were bringing in to the emergency ward.

Once the doors opened, I raced toward the gurney before the EMTs could even remove him from the ambulance to take him through another set of doors. I had been in enough hospitals to know that once he went through the next set of doors, I wouldn't be able to be with him.

I moved barely enough for the gurney and attendants to push past me.

It was Don.

I couldn't see much of Don himself. He was wearing an oxygen mask, and an IV dangled from his arm.

I needed to see him up close, to touch him, to speak to him—to do something to let him know I was there. And probably just as much to reassure myself that he was going to be all right.

Both of his legs were in the plastic, blow-up casts I'd seen put on football players who had been injured on the field. The EMTs had strapped his left arm to his chest. Don wore khaki pants that had been cut on the seams and a teal-checked Abercrombie shirt we had bought when we last visited New Orleans. It had become his favorite sport shirt.

It seems funny now, but I focused on that shirt. They had cut or torn the sleeves as well as the body of the shirt so they could take his vital signs. The shirt was covered with blood.

Don's going to be mad they cut his shirt.

It seems silly, but those were the kinds of thoughts that went through my head. They probably helped calm me.

"Do you want to talk to him?" one of the medics asked once they were inside the hospital.

I nodded gratefully, leaned over, and kissed him on the forehead. I took his hand, but he didn't respond. "Don. Don, I'm here. They're going to take good care of you."

He rolled his eyes when I called his name, but he made no effort to speak. I kept trying to reassure him by saying, "It's okay. It wasn't your fault. You're going to make it."

Later Don told me that from the way I'd stared at him, he was sure I didn't expect him to survive. He said he remembered my speaking to him, and he thought he said something to me about the accident. He didn't. He was probably conscious enough to hear but not enough to speak.

As I stared at him, I didn't see as much blood as I had expected. Of course, they had him wrapped up, but I had prepared myself for him to look worse. I pulled back but stayed next to the gurney, unsure what to do next.

"We'll be back shortly to let you know what we find out and give you an update," the medic said as he began rolling the gurney forward.

I went back into the waiting room. The two deacons were still there, along with Mark. I told them what I saw, and they were kind and sympathetic. I had mixed feelings as I spoke with the three of them. I was glad they were there because they represented our friends and members of South Park Church. But I didn't want to talk. I was aware they were trying to be encouraging and wanted to help me keep my mind off Don.

It didn't work. The more innocuous the conversation, the more my thoughts drifted back to Don. The groanings from the telephone call haunted me, but his lack of response tormented me even more.

Multiple times someone would ask if I wanted something to eat, something to drink, or perhaps a magazine to read. Each time I said, "Thank you. Not right now."

Such offers became common over the next few weeks. I've realized that when people don't know what to say or do, those are the common offerings—food, drink, or something to read.

Mark had waited, and to his credit, he didn't say much. His presence was comforting because it demanded nothing of me and yet reminded me that others cared.

I'm not sure what I expected next, but I assumed that within a few minutes the medic or a nurse would come to the waiting room and fill me in.

The wait began.

No one came.

I'm sure I was a nuisance to the woman at the admitting desk, but I couldn't seem to stop myself. Every few minutes—which seemed longer to me—I went up to her and asked, "Do we have any word yet?"

"No, ma'am, we don't."

To her credit, she didn't show impatience. She was probably used to such anxious questions from those sitting in the waiting room.

The door through which they had wheeled Don bore a sign that read Medical Personnel Only. I must have walked up to that door (which had no window) at least a dozen times. Each time I peered through the crack between the double doors, but I couldn't see much.

After about an hour I couldn't stand the tension of not knowing. Quite uncharacteristic of me, I determined to find out for myself. Turning to the men who were waiting with me, I said, "I'm going to find out what's happening." Before they could talk me out of it or I could second-guess myself, I pushed through the doors.

No one was in the hallway, but I spotted a counter and went up to it. A young intern saw me and came over to the counter. "May I help you?"

I tried to keep my voice level as I told him Don's name. "I'm trying to find out what's going on with my husband."

"No one's been out to talk to you yet?" The way he spoke told me he was surprised. After all these years, I don't remember much about his physical appearance, only that he seemed approachable and concerned.

"No, no one. I've heard nothing."

"I'm so sorry," he said, and his voice was soft and kind. He took me over to the X-ray board, where Don's X-rays were displayed. "Let me show you what's going on." He explained that Don's arm wasn't just broken, but shattered. He pointed out a number of small, jagged pieces.

Before I could say anything, he pointed to another X-ray. "This is his right knee." It looked like pictures of a jigsaw puzzle—dozens of little pieces scattered around.

He then called my attention to his left leg. "This is where the femur—the thighbone—should be."

"*Should* be?"

"Part of it's missing," he said and hurried on to the next X-ray. I learned later that four inches of the bone were missing.

"It looks as if there may be a crack in the pelvic bone, but we'll deal with that later." He pointed to the leg X-ray. "These injuries need to be attended to immediately."

Even to my untrained eye, I could tell there was nasty damage. I'd had trouble with my knees most of my life and had seen many X-rays of legs. I knew what they were supposed to look like. From that experience I could tell that his right kneecap, or patella, was going to require extensive surgery and therapy.

As the young intern explained, only tissue on the bottom of the leg connected the lower part of the left leg to the rest of his body. I was sure that was the case with his arm as well. The man also told me there was a "tremendous amount of debris inside the wound." They were going to use massive doses of antibiotics to prevent infection.

"Broken windshield glass gashed his face, and even more is lodged in his chest. We've been trying to clean that up."

Because I'm not noisy with my grief, I internalized what I saw.

I again forced myself not to cry. I stared at the X-rays, thinking how much pain Don must be feeling.

"Do you want to see him?"

"Yes, yes, please."

"Follow me." He took me down the hallway and into a room that I assumed was for pre-op patients.

The room was cold, and I shivered slightly, but my mind was on Don. He lay on a bed in the middle of the room, with a bright light shining on him. Someone had covered him with a white sheet.

The intern pulled over one of those round metal stools for me. I can still hear the sound of the legs scraping across the tile floor. I sat down, reached over, and took Don's hand.

His hand felt cold. He was pale, but I could see his chest rise and fall under the sheet. He looked peaceful.

I'd been to many funerals and seen the dead in their caskets—all four of my grandparents, a friend from church, a young woman who died from cancer—but I'd never seen anyone alive who was so pale and so still. Even after all these years, that image is so impressed on my mind that I can't forget it. Don's face and the room are as clear to me as if I just left him. The stark hospital lighting, the stainless-steel cabinets, the containers of cotton swabs, and the undeniable hospital smell made everything feel sterile and cold.

"He's not able to respond to you because he's heavily medicated," the intern said. "We couldn't give him anything until we'd done our examination."

I started to ask something about surgery or the recovery, but the words didn't come.

"They'll be coming to take him to surgery soon. They need to clean him up to avoid serious infection."

Don lay there waiting to go into surgery, and he probably wasn't aware of anything. I don't remember if there were any IVs, but I was conscious of the light and all the stainless steel. Even with my jacket, I felt chilled sitting in the room.

The intern left, I assumed, to give me a few minutes of privacy with Don.

Throughout the entire ordeal, that's the one time when the enormity of the situation hit. I felt alone, anxious, and frightened. Very frightened. It was like walking down an unlit road on a cloud-covered night. I didn't know which way to turn.

And yet, strange as it may seem, I wasn't worried about his surviving. I focused on how seriously he was injured and the pain he must have already endured.

Immediately I thought of his left leg and said to myself, *This isn't a simple fracture, and it's more than a compound fracture. His leg is missing a bone.* I knew the femur is what they call the thighbone, and it's the most important part in the leg as well as the largest bone in the body. But I still hadn't grasped the significance of that information.

Again, I focused on the shattered right kneecap, and I shivered as I thought of those tiny bone fragments inside his arm.

I'm not sure why, but until that moment I hadn't thought to ask about internal injuries. Had there been brain damage? I assumed those were things they assessed at the hospital in Huntsville. The intern had said nothing about his condition except what was in the X-rays.

That's when I cried out to God. "I'm scared. Please, please God, help me through this."

I sobbed quietly, but as soon as I calmed down, I said, "You've always taken care of us before. Take care of us here." Those simple words gave me some peace.

I had been raised in church, and prayer had been a significant part of our teaching. But I have to admit that much of my prayer had been perfunctory. I remember at times the pastor would ask certain individuals to pray aloud, and they'd go on and on. Often I tuned them out and went off on my own thoughts. Still, I prayed for my family each day, and for others. It is the right thing to do and the duty (as well as privilege) of Christians to pray for each other. Daily time in prayer and Bible reading was part of my life, so I was no stranger to talking to God.

That was before. I had never faced anything this serious. All my life I had prayed, but more often than not the prayer was general, even though it was serious: "Take care of my family; bless the missionaries; thank you for loving me." I have to confess it was done more out of routine than gut-level, painful honesty.

This prayer was different. I loved this man, the father of my children, and I didn't know what was going to happen to him. Right then, I could only think of Don's agony and his deathlike pallor. In that cold, impersonal room, prayer took on a stronger, more intense meaning for me than it had at any time in my life. I prayed, but I thought of it as more of a cry from the depth of my soul to God.

That day I faced a situation over which I had absolutely no control. I was frightened because I didn't know how to cope. I was like a child, lost at night with nothing to guide me.

I placed my head on the edge of the bed where Don lay and poured out my heart to God. I repeated and claimed the promise I heard God whisper to me in Mary Nell's office: *This will be difficult, but it's going to be okay.*

After seeing those X-rays, I had a picture of how hard it was going to be for Don. They were also the concrete evidence of what God had let me know earlier in the day—two broken legs, one broken arm.

But it's more than routine broken bones.

In the silence of that room, I prayed for myself and for Don. I prayed for the doctors who would be caring for him. I asked God to strengthen me to go through this ordeal, no matter what it took or how long. Most important, it was the first time I had ever told God how frightened I was.

Perhaps I reverted to childhood, but in those moments, more than anything else, I wanted my parents to hold me, comfort me, and assure me everything was going to be all right. I didn't want to be alone and helpless.

After I prayed several minutes, the anxieties and fears slowly dissipated. I became aware of a sense of peace as God reminded me he was my heavenly Father and was with me always. I thought of the words from the Bible, "I will never fail you. I will never abandon you" (Heb. 13:5). I don't remember saying amen, but after I raised my head, a new strength surged through me.

I was still worried about Don, and yet I was confident that God was with us and he would take both Don and me through the dark times ahead.

5.

DIFFICULT PHONE CALLS

I have no idea how long the hospital staff allowed me to sit next to Don and hold his cold, unresponsive hand. After those first few minutes alone, I'm not sure I was aware of anything except that God was with me and I sat beside my husband.

I couldn't do anything to help my husband, but I was there. Just the simple act of being able to hold Don's hand, to see his face, and to watch him breathe gave me focus. I couldn't think of what the future might hold. I focused on the next step of clearing the wounds of debris and starting antibiotics. Nothing beyond that mattered.

One step at a time. That may be a cliché, but it was real to me. It would be the way I would function over the next several days, weeks, and months as I walked through many dark places. One step at a time.

Sitting there gave me peace, and I was ready.

"Mrs. Piper," a woman's voice behind me said, "we have to take him to surgery now."

I nodded and got up. Hundreds of questions filled my mind, but I didn't know how to ask.

"We're going to get him cleaned up," a nurse told me. "We need to disinfect these wounds and get him stabilized."

She probably said more, but that's all I could absorb. I felt as if I couldn't move. I couldn't do anything except stare at her.

"You need to go to the main waiting room," she said.

I nodded, but still seemed unable and unwilling to move.

She gently took my arm and turned me toward the door.

I no longer felt any fear or anxiety. No emotion. Everything was out of my hands, and I could do nothing.

I was numb.

———

After the nurse took me out of the room, I stood beside the door that led back into the waiting room and watched the staff wheel Don through another set of doors. I was still numb, but I could feel the terror and panic trying to push to the surface. Not wanting to fall apart in front of the men who had come to be with me, I took several deep breaths to calm myself and regain the peace I had felt earlier. By the time I had gone back through the double doors and into the waiting room, I was once again in control of my emotions.

The two deacons and Mark were still sitting there. They stood as I came toward them. I asked them to sit down and related what little I knew. I was careful not to tell them how scared I had felt. Maybe that was part of protective-mother mode. Or maybe it was too private and too personal to share.

I think there was a brief silence—although I'm not sure—before one of the deacons blurted out, "Eva, you need to have something to eat."

"Why don't we go to the cafeteria?" the second one asked. "I'll let the nurse know where we'll be."

I must have agreed to go because the next thing I remember is sitting in the empty cafeteria, trying to force myself to eat a salad and drink a Diet Coke while the men around me tried to offer comfort.

Because Mark was the father of young children, I urged him to go home.

"It's all right. I can stay—"

"No, really, I'm doing okay," I said. "Please go home. I'll find a way to get back to Alvin."

He protested, but once I assured him I was all right and someone would take me home when I was ready to go, he left.

When I had finished eating—although I left most of the salad—we walked back to the main waiting area. At the time, Hermann Hospital was undergoing a massive remodeling, so the normal surgical waiting room was unusable. Instead someone directed us to the front lobby. The ER nurse had told me I would get word there when Don was out of surgery.

It was a large room with lots of cold, impersonal tile. The massive front doors opened onto the steps leading into the hospital. I stared at rows and rows of dark-blue seats of imitation leather. The seats were attached in sets of seven or eight with a metal armrest separating each chair from the next.

Along one wall was a bank of pay phones. The wall was around a corner, which meant it did provide some form of privacy even though voices seemed to echo into the lobby.

I realized I needed to let the children know what was going on, so I called the Chisolms' home. By then it was about nine o'clock, which meant church was over. As soon as the phone rang, Kim's mother answered.

I briefly explained what little I knew and that I had seen Don. Then I asked to speak to Nicole. I explained to my daughter as best I could that I had seen her daddy and that he was in surgery. I promised to call her at school the next day to give her an update. We exchanged "I love yous" and said good night.

Next I called Susan Long, who told me the boys were fine. She said that when they got to her house, Joe went outside and played with her children, who were around the same age. Before Chris went out to play, however, he wanted to look at her anatomy book, so she could show him which of his dad's bones were broken. That's how Chris processes information: he needs to have the details.

Susan ended the call by telling me the boys were asleep and she would take them to school the next day.

After checking in on the kids, I needed to let my parents know what was happening. As I fished through my purse for the paper bag of change, I asked myself, *Whom should I call? Whom do I need to contact to let know what's going on?*

I pulled out the brown bag and laid the coins out in small stacks. I decided to call my mom and dad first. I gave the long-distance operator the number, inserted the coins in the slot, and listened to the *ching* as each coin was automatically counted.

While I waited for the phone to ring at the other end, I silently thanked God that I had the change and for impressing upon me to bring the coins.

I needed to talk to my parents; perhaps I was reverting emotionally back to my dependency on them when I was a child. I didn't try to figure it out—I just needed to talk to the two people who had been my emotional anchor before Don came into my life. Everything was purely instinctive.

As soon as Dad answered, I blurted out, "Don's been in an accident! A terrible accident!"

"Just a minute. I need to get your mother on the phone."

There was a click when Mom picked up the extension.

Dad's calm voice had exactly the effect on me that I needed. After I told them what little I knew, he said, "We're not able to leave tonight, but we'll pack up and take off first thing in the morning."

With great dread I called Don's mother, Billie. She's strong in many ways and yet fragile in others and can be extremely emotional. "First, everything is going to be all right," I said, careful not to betray any emotion. "Don's been in a serious accident."

"How serious?"

"Very." I told her what little I knew.

Billie reacted exactly as I expected: she screamed.

Don's father, Ralph, grabbed the phone. He was calmer, as I assumed he would be. I told him everything I knew. As I spoke, I wondered how many times I'd have to repeat the meager amount of information I knew.

"We'll be there as soon as we can make arrangements," he said. "We'll have to get someone to handle the animals, but we'll be down there as soon as we can."

I talked to my parents again a few minutes later, and they decided to wait until Friday so Don's mother could ride with them. Don's father wouldn't be able to arrive until Sunday. I thanked them for setting aside everything else. It's a long drive from Bossier City—about five hours—so they would reach Houston sometime Friday afternoon.

With those calls made, I felt more relaxed—especially because I was able to speak to Dad.

I'm able to cope. I can do it.

———

While I had been speaking with my parents, the other pay phones had begun to ring, and the callers asked to speak to me. News was spreading about the accident, and people were calling to get information. The two deacons jumped in to answer phone calls and dispense the latest news. I appreciated that.

Soon we were getting calls not only from Alvin but from back home in Bossier City as well. If the call was from someone the deacons felt I would want to talk to, such as a close family friend or relative, they handed me the phone. Otherwise they took on the role of a press corps, sharing what they knew and asking for prayer.

Between calls, I tried to think of who else I needed to contact. I took a few deep breaths and sorted out the names of the people I should call. None of our lifelong friends lived in our calling area, so I was once again grateful for the small sack of coins.

I started calling Don's close friends. David Gentiles and Cliff McArdle were first because they were Don's best friends.

I smiled as I thought about Don, David, and Cliff together. Several times I had jokingly referred to them as the holy trinity. They had been close and had known one another since their early ministry years in Bossier City. All three had become Baptist ministers in the Northwest Louisiana region.

David had followed Don as youth minister at Barksdale Baptist Church, while Don continued on in a volunteer position. They had worked in tandem, planning and organizing events for the youth. Although Don has two brothers, David was his closest friend and confidant. They talked about everything. Cliff had served at a church about an hour away, but they still got together as often as possible. All were huge LSU fans (except when LSU played Alabama, Cliff's home state) and enjoyed either watching games on TV or occasionally finding tickets to attend in person. They had a special bond as men and as ministers.

During the past two years, all three had moved to Texas. Cliff and Don were both in the greater Houston area; David was living in San Antonio.

When I called Cliff, his wife, Suzanne, answered. Her husband wasn't home, but she listened and expressed her concern. Before we finished the call, Suzanne said she'd contact Cliff right way and also promised, "I'll get the word to others."

I also called Darrell Guyton and Bill Jones. They were two of our close friends from Bossier City. Don had known them and their wives, Karen and Terri, since high school. We had enjoyed many activities together as young married couples.

Darrell had been Don's roommate in college. (In fact, we named one of our twins, Joseph Darrell, after him.) While in school Darrell had lost his father in a car accident. More recently, his sister had survived a serious car accident. If anyone would understand how I felt, Darrell would.

Except for my parents and David Gentiles, I gave the briefest details in my telephone calls—it was all I knew anyway. Most of the time I kept it simple: "Don has been in a serious accident. They have him in surgery right now." I then gave a quick rundown of the injuries I knew about and concluded with, "I covet your prayers. I'll let you know as soon as we know more details."

By the time I had called David and talked with Suzanne, I had made a mental list of other people to notify. That action kept me focused on the calls and pushed my mind away from Don and his surgery. I phoned people from the school and church. I also tried to think of friends in Alvin to call for prayer that Don would make it through the surgery safely, which I thoroughly expected him to do.

In my mind I pictured the next day, when a nurse or doctor would come into his room and say, "He'll have to be here a week or two, but he's doing just fine." I would smile and thank God for the good news.

That's what played inside my head.

My thinking was a long, long way from reality.

6.
THE FIRST DAY

After perhaps another hour, the door opened, and I looked up to see Cliff McArdle walking toward me. The concern on his face was as important as any words he could say.

He grabbed me in his arms. "I'm sorry. I'm so sorry."

Having known Cliff longer than I had known any of the other people in the room, I found that his quick embrace and his few words brought immense comfort. In those moments I realized how deep his friendship was with Don. Even though I was still walking in darkness, I knew God had sent someone to be with me, at least for a short time.

I made introductions and continued answering and making phone calls. As I would learn, the need to call others becomes overpowering to those of us in waiting rooms. It may be a way to relieve our anxiety because it means doing something—something sensible and tangible. It also takes our minds off our loved ones.

Momentarily. Then reality sets in again.

Eventually the frequency of phone calls decreased. I sat down in one of the chairs closest to the wall in case a phone rang. My head was in my hands as I tried to relax. I sensed someone sitting next to me. Looking up, I saw Stan Mauldin, my friend Suzan's husband.

Stan and I talked for several minutes, but afterward I could remember nothing except that he offered to drive me home. "I need to stay here," I said. "There's nothing I can do for Don, but I need to be here anyway."

He was sensitive enough that I didn't have to explain. I *had* to stay at the hospital. Maybe I had to be there mostly for myself, as if I could make things better with my presence. I wanted to know immediately about any changes in Don's condition, and if I left, I'd worry about him the whole time.

"I'll spend the night here," I said. "I'm sure I can figure out a place to sleep." I assured Stan that I was all right and there wasn't anything new to report. "I'll call you and Suzan as soon as they tell me any news."

Stan is a big man. He once played on a national championship football team for the University of Texas and was the head football coach of Alvin High School. While his physical size is impressive, what draws most people to him are his soft Texas drawl and his caring heart. If Stan knew someone needed something, he would be the first one there to help, no matter what.

He hugged me gently, expressed his love for both Don and me, and left.

Cliff talked with the others who were still there. I'm grateful that he took command of the conversation so I wouldn't have to keep talking.

After a while Cliff said, "It's getting late. You need to eat." I suspect one of the deacons had told him I had barely touched my salad earlier.

"I'm not hungry."

"I'll stay right here," Cliff said. "Please get yourself some food from the cafeteria, or at least from the vending machines." Those words and the gesture were so characteristic of Cliff. "If there is any word, I'll come and get you immediately—"

I shook my head. "I'm not hungry."

"That may be true," he said, "but you still need to get something."

As he stared at me, I knew it was useless to argue. I nodded and tried to smile.

I got up and one of the others led me to the vending area. I selected something, probably Cheese Nips, but I honestly had no appetite. I felt I had to get back to the waiting room, even though there wasn't a thing I could do.

The intern had promised that as soon as Don was out of surgery, someone would give me a report on his condition. I hoped there would be some news by the time we returned to the waiting room.

No news. No nurse or intern had come.

I had no way to know that the surgery would take eleven hours. I had been at the hospital fewer than three hours, and no one was providing any updates. It felt like an endless night of waiting.

I kept urging the people from the church not to stay. "Who knows how long it will be?" After I'd said it several times, most of them decided to leave, singly or in small groups.

"We're going to go home," they each said in different ways. "Call us if you need anything."

I promised I would.

"I'm not leaving," Cliff said matter-of-factly. That was his way of saying, "It's not worth arguing over, because I've made up my mind."

———

Shortly after midnight Cliff said softly, "You need to get some sleep."

I looked around. The room may have worked well for short-term waiting, but it wasn't equipped for sleeping. "I don't think I can."

"You'll figure it out," he said.

I was tired, but I wasn't ready to sleep; yet I decided I needed to try. Cliff would hover over me until I did.

I gazed around the room, which was probably an atrium. Rows of metal chairs with hard cushions and metal armrests all locked together didn't look inviting to anyone who wanted to sleep. There was no way to get comfortable, but I did my best by putting my legs under an armrest. Probably more from exhaustion than anything else, I did sleep a little.

As he promised, Cliff stayed the entire night.

Every time someone came into the room, I woke up; Cliff would still be alert. One couple came in because their son had flipped his pickup and was seriously injured. Although they were quiet, I could still hear them talk between themselves and to Cliff about the seriousness of the accident. I would soon learn and appreciate that camaraderie develops with people who are thrown together following life-threatening accidents of loved ones.

As the couple continued to talk, I gave up any attempt to sleep and joined Cliff in talking with them. The couple told me what they knew about their son, and I shared with them my reason for being there.

Before long a nurse came into the waiting room and walked over to the couple. "Your son is out of surgery," she said and took them to see him. I would see them again several times because their boy was assigned to the bed, or "pod," next to Don in the ICU.

I still hadn't heard anything about Don. I tried not to feel concerned, but it was difficult not to wonder, and the anxiety crept back inside me.

I'm not sure of the time, but I could see the first rays of the sun when a doctor came into the waiting room and went to the information desk that served as the nurses' station. His back was to me, but after the nurse pointed to me, he turned around and nodded to me.

At last, I thought, *I'm going to get some news.*

He was wearing green scrubs, and I remember that he was a

short man and had a moustache. He sat down and put his hand on my right knee, "I'm Dr. Tom Greider, an orthopedic surgeon. I'm so sorry to have to meet you under these circumstances." He explained that they had worked all night on Don, which is why I had heard nothing.

All night?

I couldn't begin to comprehend what kind of surgery they performed on my husband, but the kindness in the doctor's voice touched me and finally pushed aside my confusion.

"The best news is that we see no evidence of brain trauma or internal injuries."

I smiled gratefully at that small bit of good news. Afterward, when I saw Don, as well as pictures of the car, I could hardly believe there had been no brain damage after what he had gone through.

Dr. Greider went on to explain that he had started with the kneecap in Don's right leg. The left forearm had to be stabilized—I wasn't sure what that meant—because those bones were in so many pieces. "We've put his left leg into traction." He paused and stared at me. "Four and a half inches of the femur is missing."

"I saw the X-ray," I said.

"Then you know," he said. "We put a basket on his right knee."

I nodded. Even though I understood what a basket was, he described it as something like a wire mesh net. "It's like a basket because it holds those pieces together."

His explanation went on for several minutes, and by then I understood why Don's surgery had lasted so many hours. Whenever Dr. Greider felt I didn't understand something, he didn't seem to mind clarifying before he continued with the next bit of information.

"In a little while they'll take him up to the intensive care unit." He told me it was a new unit, and Don would be one of the first patients they placed in that pod. He then stated that the orthopedic injuries were "pretty nasty" and that I should expect a long recovery for Don.

Dr. Greider gave me such a sense of comfort. First of all, for him to sit down beside me and say, "I'm so sorry about this," touched me.

Other surgeons I've met have been brusque and in a hurry when they explained the condition—if I could stop them long enough to get information. Dr. Greider had a warm, caring persona. I liked him the minute I met him; and in the days ahead, I was to learn that my first impressions were correct.

His last words before leaving filled me with confidence and encouragement. "We're going to take care of him," he said, and smiled. "And he's going to be okay."

I thanked him.

"Your husband is still in recovery. In about an hour you can go up to the ICU and see him." Then he stood, looked into my eyes, and said, "You need to rest. Why don't you get some sleep?"

As he walked away, I said to myself, "Yeah, right. How and where do I do that?"

After Dr. Greider left, Cliff and I looked at each other and smiled. Both of us felt a sense of relief. We walked over to the nurses' station. "I understand my husband is now in recovery," I said to the nurse on duty. "Where can I wait for him?"

"He'll be going into ICU in a few minutes. We've already assigned him a room when he comes out of ICU," the nurse replied. "If you want to go up to his room and wait for him, that's all right." Then she smiled at me and said, "You look tired. You can lie down in his bed until we call you."

"Thank you," I answered. It was about eight thirty the morning after the wreck, and exhaustion had crept through my entire body. Now that I knew more, I was able to relax.

Cliff also thanked her and said, "We'll go up there now." He took my arm and led me to the elevators. We went into Don's assigned room. "You do need to lie down for a while."

Exhausted as I was, I protested.

"They said they would come get you when it's time to see Don," Cliff reminded me. "I'll stop at the nurses' station on the floor to make sure they know where you are."

He was ready to leave, and I thanked him. His presence had made the long night much easier.

Cliff left shortly after that because he planned to go on to work. But he refused to leave the hospital until he made sure I was lying in the bed.

I must have fallen asleep almost immediately. I hadn't had any real sleep since Tuesday night, and it was now Thursday morning. My next moment of awareness was a nurse gently shaking me. She pulled me out of a deep cavern of much-needed sleep. I stared at my watch and realized that I had had an hour to an hour and a half of sleep. That wasn't nearly enough, but I felt better.

The nurse let me know I could see Don.

Before I could head for the ICU, John Higgins from our church came to the room where I was resting. John had some connections to the Texas Department of Public Safety; he had checked into the accident and was able to fill me in on details.

"Yes, it was an eighteen-wheeler," he said, "driven by an inmate from the state prison." The prison, the Ellis Unit, was fewer than five miles from the other end of the bridge, the way Don had been headed. The inmate had volunteered to drive the truck after the regular driver hadn't shown up, which was possibly the reason for the accident. Driving a huge truck like that isn't as easy as it may look, especially on a rain-soaked, narrow bridge.

Don had been wearing a seat belt; otherwise the injuries would have been even more severe. Two other cars were involved in the accident, John told me, but no one else had been injured.

John offered to go with me to the ICU. I had no idea how to get there, so it was an easy decision to accept his offer. He had a take-charge attitude about him and was familiar with Hermann Hospital. As we walked down the hallway together, I made note of landmarks so I could find my way back on my own.

John and I arrived at Don's ICU pod around ten that morning. The staff didn't have to tell me the unit was new. Not only were all the colors fresh and the carpets just laid, but the odor of paint lingered in the hallways.

As in other hospitals, the ICU allows visitors to see patients for only five or ten minutes at a time. Usually staff will allow a visitor or two every hour as they did in Hermann from midmorning until midafternoon.

Both of us were able to go into the unit. Don was hooked up to a variety of IVs and machines. The *dit-dit-dit* sound was one of the first things that grabbed my attention. One time an alarm went off, and a nurse hurried into the pod to increase the oxygen flow. At the time I wasn't aware—and they were careful not to tell me—that he was on a life-support apparatus. For me, the room was a blur of dials, gadgets, and strange sounds.

Some kind of monitor, a pulse oximeter, was fastened to my husband's right index finger to check oxygen flow. Pulleys, hung on the end of the bed, were attached to his left leg, while the right was immobilized with large bandages.

That's when I saw the terrible marks where doctors had removed glass from his face. What really caught my eye was the bruise that ran from his left shoulder across his chest where the seat belt had held him in place. The injured spot was just beginning to turn blue, but there was no mistaking what made that mark.

How violent the impact must have been to leave that distinct of a bruise, I thought, and closed my eyes against that picture.

Occasionally Don moaned, and I cringed inside. No sound disturbed me more than Don's moans through the oxygen mask.

As it had been in the pre-op room in the ER, being in this room with Don brought me great comfort. It was as if my being with him would give him strength; at least that's how I felt. It was emotionally painful to observe his lying there with all those tubes, unable to move. The severity of his injuries still hadn't sunk in. Right then, I was thankful he was alive and breathing.

The pod itself was defined by curtains hanging on both sides.

Don's hospital bed backed up against a wall holding the typical hospital equipment. Other machines surrounded his bed, with tubes and wires running from them to various places on Don's body. The fourth side of the pod had another curtain that opened into the ICU main area, where the nurses' station was located.

I stared at him, trying to absorb everything. His left forearm was wrapped up so that it looked huge. His left leg was in traction, with wires holding it up. It was elevated with what looked like a piece of canvas under the leg, fastened to a metal frame. That frame was attached to an overhead pulley that held a weight dangling from the foot of the bed. Don's leg was wrapped in layer after layer of ACE bandages to stabilize it in place of the missing femur.

I saw what I wanted to see—a simple broken leg—even though the intern had shown me the X-rays and I had talked with Dr. Greider that morning.

As I'd done the night before, I leaned over and kissed Don's forehead and called him by name. His eyelids fluttered a few times, which made me assume he heard me but couldn't respond. He seemed to breathe normally, which was a relief.

I talked as calmly and as casually as I could to him. Even though he didn't react, I wanted to make sure he knew I loved him and that many, many people were praying for him. I'd been told years earlier that even when patients don't seem to respond, they often hear what others say. I wanted him to hear the love in my voice.

Just then, a nurse came into the room and checked his vital signs. She said softly, "He's stable. We have him on the traction to keep the leg in one position."

She didn't tell me why that was so important—and I had no hint of the seriousness of his situation. Dr. Greider had mentioned the loss of the femur, but the information hadn't yet sunk in that he couldn't go on that way indefinitely.

We were probably in there for the entire ten minutes, but time seemed to have no relevance. John and I kept talking to Don in quiet

voices, assuring him everything was going to be all right. I placed my
hand around his to let him know I was there. I told him repeatedly that I
loved him, that the kids loved him, and that people were praying for him.

I didn't cry because I didn't want to upset him, although he did
nothing to show he was aware I was there. I tried to send him strength
through my words and my touch. Don had always been the strong
one; now it was my turn.

A nurse opened the front curtain and said, "It's time to leave."

I kissed Don again and walked out of his room. I hurt for him
and tried not to think of what he'd have to go through to recover.
Looking back, I'm glad I didn't know how bad he was.

John left me outside the ICU, and I went back to the hospital
room by myself. As far as I can remember, I laid on the bed again and
went to sleep.

A knock on the door startled me, and a man entered, asking for
a patient. The same nurse who had awakened me earlier came up
behind him to tell him the patient he wanted to see would be moved
to the room shortly. I began to gather my things to leave.

I must have looked confused because the nurse said to me, "Mr.
Piper has been assigned to a different room. You can wait there." She
didn't make it clear how long I could wait, but I ended up staying in
the room from that Thursday morning until the following Tuesday.
I appreciated her kindness and expressed my gratitude as I walked
around the corner to the new room.

At the time I didn't realize it, but we would eventually be charged for
both the ICU and a regular room. The hospital puts their most severely
ill patients in ICU and reserves a private room at the same time. That
way, when a patient is ready to leave the ICU, the attending physicians
have a place to send him, and he doesn't have to stay any longer than
necessary in the intensive care unit. Even though it cost extra, I felt it
was a good idea. Besides, medical expenses and who would pay them
were nowhere in my thoughts. I became aware of the double charge
only later, when I received the first bill.

———

Don made it through the day on Thursday and all through the night. Reminding myself of that fact gave me additional encouragement. No one said it, but I assumed that every hour he survived meant he was improving.

Because I had seen the X-rays after he was admitted, I knew it was a serious matter, but I still had no idea that his injuries were life threatening. Even Dr. Greider hadn't said that. Perhaps he was trying to be kind and not cause me additional worries. Or perhaps he was so determined to keep Don alive that he wouldn't allow negative results to invade his thoughts.

In my naïveté I still assumed the doctors would put a cast on his leg and do a few other things, and then he'd improve and come home. I was willing to admit that it might be three weeks or even a month, but I couldn't conceive of any time longer than that. How could I have known that Don would have to have more than twenty surgeries within one year?

Other surgeries followed, and Don underwent a total of thirty-four operations as part of his recovery. Not only could I not have fathomed that number, but I'm not sure I could have stood up emotionally had I known.

7.

THE CHILDREN SEE
THEIR FATHER

M y parents drove to Alvin and stayed at our house. That way, our three children could stay at home with them at night. Mom and Dad also spent as much time as they could with me in the hospital. It meant so much to me to have them beside me. But more important, I knew the kids were safe.

After five days the children still hadn't seen Don, and I felt they needed to come to the hospital and see him for themselves. I also felt it would cheer Don up if they came. I talked to the staff, and our doctors agreed. On Monday after school Mom and Dad brought the kids to the hospital.

Before they went in to visit Don, a child psychologist on staff asked me if he could talk to the children and prepare them for what they'd encounter.

"Yes, please do," I said. "I think it will help all of us to go through this better."

The psychologist brought our children and me into a room while my parents waited in the hall outside the ICU. Once we were seated, he brought out a dummy. "Before you see your father, I want to show you what's wrong with him." Then he explained everything in simple, easy-to-understand language and made certain the children grasped the seriousness of their father's situation. I felt relieved because I wouldn't have been able to explain most of what he said. In fact, I learned a few things myself.

I thanked the psychologist before I took the children to the ICU. I wanted the meeting to be only the five of us—Don, me, Chris, Joe, and Nicole. Don was conscious and alert enough to know we were there.

Don was still hooked up to so many machines and devices there was no way any of us could hug him. Nicole was tall enough to see him in the raised bed, but the boys were barely able to see his face.

"I love you, Daddy," Nicole said, and she touched his arm.

He nodded and mumbled, "I love you too." The words weren't distinct but were clear enough that we understood.

The boys said the same thing, and both times Don responded. His words alone weren't much, but they were still a response. And each response strengthened us.

The children handled the situation quite well, and I was grateful for the psychologist's preparation. We stayed the allotted ten minutes. During that time the children talked to their dad cheerfully, as only kids can. I was proud of them for sharing the little events of their lives and acting as if the situation were otherwise quite normal. I don't know how much he understood, and that probably wasn't important.

They were there. That was important. I know their presence comforted and encouraged Don.

After the nurse told us our time was up, each of us expressed our love, and the kids left the ICU to wait in the hallway with my parents. After the kids left, I went back to see Don, to tell him good night, and to say, "I'll see you in the morning."

He was awake and more alert this time. Tears filled his eyes. "We have great kids, don't we?" It was the best, most positive thing Don had said to me since the accident.

I began to cry. "Yeah, we do." As I said that, I thought of something Don had said to me many times: "We have better kids than we deserve."

I could tell the visit had taken a lot out of him, so I told him to rest and I would see him in the morning. I brushed the tears from my eyes before I walked out of the ICU. I didn't want the kids to see me crying and think something was wrong.

We exchanged hugs, and then I watched as the kids walked down the hall with their grandparents. I assumed they had understood and were assured that Don was going to improve.

Only years later would my father tell me the truth. "Chris and Nicole both thought their dad was doing to die." I must have looked shocked because he said, "They told me."

"I'm glad I didn't know how they felt," I said, "or I would have worried about them as well as Don."

———

I had not left the hospital since the afternoon of the accident almost a week earlier. It was a dark time, and about to get darker. By then the doctors knew, as all of us did, that it wasn't going to be a fast recovery.

Instead of weeks, hospital staff were using the word *months*.

8.

"THE CHILDREN NEED YOU!"

Don's accident had happened on a Wednesday, and my parents had come to Houston on Friday. They'd brought Don's mother with them.

Dad was a high school assistant principal, and he'd had to make preparations before he could leave Bossier City, which is why it took them a full day to get there. They stayed at our house and took care of all three children.

Their presence was comforting and probably the first time I felt I could truly be myself around anyone after the accident. When they came to the hospital, I didn't have to entertain them or try to make them feel I was doing well.

The following week—I don't remember which day—my mother called me at the hospital and made it clear that I needed to come home because the children needed me. "You belong here with them. They can take care of Don at the hospital. They'll call you if they need you there."

"I need to be here—"

"You *need* to be with your children."

"I can't talk about this right now. I'll see what I can do."

After hanging up I fell apart. I knew my mom's heart. She wasn't intentionally putting an extra burden on me. All through her adult life, her children and now her grandchildren were her first concern. In her eyes I needed to get out of the hospital to get some rest, and my kids needed their mom.

Several times I had considered the same thing. How could I be with Don and yet be at home, an hour's drive away? I was the oldest child in the family and, like many firstborns, I became the responsible one to help care for the younger ones.

This isn't to blame anyone, only to say that I was torn over what I was *supposed* to do. I felt everyone needed a piece of me, and there wasn't anything left for me. Everyone else seemed to know what I needed to do. So why didn't I?

I've always tried to please my parents, and I wanted to do what my mom insisted, but I could not—absolutely could not—leave the hospital. I didn't know if Don needed me, and his lack of response didn't make it any easier. As much as I loved my three children (and was sure they understood), my place was to stay beside my husband.

Still I asked myself, *Is Mom right?* I couldn't be in both places, and I couldn't care for them adequately without neglecting Don.

"I don't know what to do," I moaned. "Lord, please, please help me." I understood what people meant when they referred to a basket case. That described me. I was hurt that Mom didn't seem to understand my need to be with Don, and I was angry at Don's lack of response. I felt no appreciation for what I was trying to do.

Does he care whether I'm here? Would he like it better if I stayed away?

I was confused, and I didn't know what to do. How could I honor my mother's demand for me to return home and still be with Don?

In the midst of trying to decide what to do, my only sister, Kaye, arrived from Austin. She and I were both born on Thanksgiving Day, two years apart. When we were younger, we shared a room, toys, and our birthday parties. Over the years our different interests had led us on separate paths. We saw each other on holidays when we would all gather at my parents' home, but that was about it. I wouldn't say we were close, but we still had that sister bond.

My parents coming to Houston was the first important and comforting thing that stood out during that period. Kaye was the second.

"Mom insists I come home," I cried to my sister, "but I just can't leave, no matter how Don responds—or doesn't respond. I don't know what to do."

Kaye hugged me, comforted me, and listened to me spill out my conflicted feelings. When I stopped talking, she did something quite startling. She picked up the phone and called my parents at my house. I was in a different room, so she had to tell me later what she said.

"Eva is not coming home," Kaye told Mom. "She knows the children need her, but this is her place. She belongs here at the hospital with Don. She has all she can handle right now."

She refused to tell me what Mom said, only that she agreed.

"Everything is fine," Kaye said to me. "She understands that you need to be here."

I felt such strong relief. I had been struggling to hold myself together, and my mother's demand threw me into the proverbial tailspin. If Kaye hadn't been there and come to my defense, I don't know what I would have done.

It wasn't a matter of screaming or yelling. The darkness hit me from all sides. Worse, it seemed as if people were pulling at me from behind and in front, and I couldn't move.

Despite my resolve, everyone was telling me what I needed to do. That's an exaggeration, but it felt that way. No one asked me what I wanted to do. Even if they had, I had no idea how I would have answered except to say, "I belong here, with my husband." It was the right place for me.

9.

OUR FIRST DISAGREEMENT

I think your mother and I should take the twins home with us," Dad said. "We'll enroll them at a nearby school so you won't have to worry about whether they're taken care of."

Dad was wise, and I knew it, but it was still difficult to let our sons go with them to live so far away. I did need to be able to concentrate on Don, so it seemed the sensible thing to do.

It was also emotionally challenging, which is another thing I learned to accept. Sometimes the right thing is the most painful. The boys would be loved and taken care of, and because they'd be with their grandparents, they would worry less about their dad.

My mind agreed; my heart ached.

"It won't be long. Just until Don recovers enough to leave the hospital," my father said, adding, "That way you can focus fully on caring for Don."

"Let me talk to Don first," I said.

It was a difficult time for Don and me with very limited communication. Don was still in ICU and was barely conscious most of the time. At first I didn't know if it took too much energy for him to talk or if he just didn't want to talk to anyone, including me.

"Hello. How are you doing today?" I'd ask. "How are you feeling?"

No matter what I said to him, I received little response. He usually kept his eyes closed. He'd nod or perhaps shake his head. He spoke few words during that period.

Finally, I decided I had to tell him about Dad's offer to care for the twins. I took a deep breath before I said, "My dad thinks it would be better if they took the boys back to Louisiana with them, until we can get you out of the hospital."

"I don't think that's a very good idea."

"I know, but it would be better for the boys, because that way I don't have to keep finding people to take them to school and pick them up."

I don't know what went on inside Don. He was filled with medication, and he was anything but his old self, so his saying little didn't bother me very much.

Not then.

He might have said another sentence or two; I don't recall. I remember that no matter what I said, I received a negative response, either he'd grunt or he'd turn his face away.

I tried to reason with him and to explain how impossible it was for me to return to teaching school, still spend so much time with him, and have energy and time to care for our children. As I talked I realized that letting my parents take the kids was the only sensible solution, but I wanted Don to agree. I knew I'd feel at peace if we both agreed to allow the boys to go.

He didn't say yes. He finally said, "Hmm."

I don't think he had the energy to argue or discuss the matter as he would have in normal times.

I kept trying to reason with him, while on some level I understood how he felt. Even though he could do nothing to care for our sons, he wanted them there. Don later told me that one of the only things he could count on at that time was the love and presence of our kids and me.

Perhaps sending them away made him feel as if it were one more thing over which he had no control. However, I knew sending the twins with my parents was the best solution for all of us. Don is a strong person, and I usually acquiesced to him. Although it was difficult, I finally made the decision to send the boys home with Mom and Dad. It broke my heart to see the pain in his eyes when I told him they were leaving. Yet I still knew I'd made the right decision.

"I'm sending Joe and Chris home with my parents," I said.

Don didn't say anything.

I was learning to walk down the dark path one step at a time. It didn't get easier, but I was growing stronger.

For a few minutes feelings of guilt overwhelmed me, but I had so many things on my mind and heart, I spent little time rethinking what I had done. I made a decision that I believed then (and still do today) was right. I had to take some kind of action to provide for the boys.

Even though I couldn't keep the family together, it was the best temporary solution and what I needed to do. I love my children; however, my first responsibility was Don, and my desire was to focus on his recovery. Everything else was secondary.

"It's fine for you to take the boys," I told Dad. I thanked my parents because it wouldn't be easy to have two second-grade boys in their house. My siblings and I had long been out of the house. As my dad said, "We're not spring chickens anymore," but they saw our need and stepped in to fill a gap. I couldn't have done it without them.

I still cried when they left.

Nicole was a different situation. Stan and Suzan Mauldin offered to take care of her. "She can live with us for now," Suzan said. Stan and Suzan were the parents of two children: Laura, a daughter close to Nicole's age; and a younger son, Bradley.

"She's over at our place, and she's doing fine with Laura," Stan said. "She knows our routine, so it's not much of an adjustment."

"She won't be any trouble," Suzan assured me. "You don't need to worry about Nicole. Do what you absolutely have to do at the hospital, and don't be concerned."

I felt grateful. Nicole had started junior high and had only four months to finish the school year. For her it would have been a big deal to move to another school temporarily.

Another factor also came into play. Nicole is a little stubborn, a trait she probably learned from her mother. Before she knew the Mauldins had offered to take her to live with them, she said, "I'm not leaving. I'm staying in the house. Alone."

She wanted to be close to her daddy and felt she was old enough. She was not only our firstborn but she had always been close to her father, so I couldn't deprive her of the ability to stay nearby. But however grown-up she assumed she might be, staying at home alone was not an option. I agreed to let her stay with the Mauldins.

Don's car wreck had far-reaching effects on all of us then, and they extend even to today. It was years before Nicole told me how alone she had felt away from home. Her brothers had their grandparents, and I had Don. She'd been with a family, but it wasn't her own. It hurt to hear those words, but I still believe it was the best solution at the time.

The care for all three children was settled, so I could focus my full attention on Don, who was still in ICU. He still had a long way to go and many, many months of pain to endure. The darkness continued to build.

10.
Dealing with a Lawyer

I constantly walked in the dark and stumbled onto things I had never thought about before. One of the big issues was people insisting that I had to hire a lawyer. I didn't even know how to contact a good attorney.

I prayed for guidance, and before I was ready to act, God answered.

John Higgins, the man who went to the ICU with me the first time, recommended a lawyer from the Beaumont area who dealt with cases of severe accidents like Don's. "He's an expert," our friend said, "and a man of integrity."

I took John's recommendation. On January 20 I called the law offices, and after I explained our situation, one of their lawyers agreed to handle our case. He helped with the initial filing and other legal issues.

One of the first things our newly hired attorney said was, "You need to take pictures so we'll have a record of Don's progress." He pointed out that we might have to prove how badly Don was injured, and the ongoing pictures would follow his progress.

That was an excellent idea, and we did exactly what he told us.

We retained a lawyer for two reasons. First, Don had been hit with a state truck from the prison, which was driven by an inmate. Letting the inmate get behind the wheel wasn't illegal, but it was a poor choice to allow an inexperienced, untested driver to take the wheel of an eighteen-wheeler.

Several of our friends were concerned that there might be a cover-up or that the State of Texas would try to deny that an inmate had driven the truck or attempt to alter the circumstances surrounding the accident. So hiring a lawyer seemed wise to me. To our relief, the state never denied their fault in the accident.

Second, I was sure Don's ongoing medical costs were going to be astronomical, and we didn't have the resources to pay those bills.

Darrell Guyton, our friend from Bossier City whose sister had been in a serious car accident, talked to me about the importance of securing financial help for Don's medical care both then and in the future. That was another factor in making the decision to hire an attorney.

I could never have dealt with all the legal forms or stood up intelligently in defending our case. Having our lawyer represent us lifted a heavy load off of me. I felt at peace knowing that someone else was thinking ahead and was concerned about our legal rights.

On January 19, the morning after Don's surgery, the hospital allowed me to stay in a lovely, spacious private room they had reserved for Don. I stayed there until January 24, when a nurse knocked on the door and told me I had to leave. "I'm sorry, but we need the room for another patient." She explained that because they didn't know when Don would leave the ICU, the room had been assigned to another patient.

If I hadn't already engaged a lawyer, I'm not sure what I would have done. Immediately I phoned our attorney and said, "They want me to leave the hospital. I don't want to do that. To drive home means at least a forty-five-minute trip." I couldn't imagine being that far away from Don or having to drive that distance every day.

Although my voice was calm, I wanted to scream, "What else can go wrong?"

Our lawyer went to work. Within half an hour he told me he had arranged a place for me to stay and that it was paid for through their law offices.

I was relieved. He had booked a room at the Downtown Marriott until Don was moved from the ICU. There was one good thing for me about the new arrangement: I had a bed in which to sleep—a real bed. Don stayed in the ICU for nearly two weeks.

———

It was a short walk, about four city blocks, to the hospital each morning and back again in the evening. I never felt uncomfortable walking, as both the hotel and the hospital faced Fannin, one of Houston's main streets. I actually enjoyed the walk because it gave me a chance to get out for some fresh air to clear my head.

"Surely, we're over the worst," I said to myself several times.

———

The day after I moved into the hotel, I faced the worst part of Don's recovery.

Complications set in following what was to have been a simple surgery the previous day. When he came out of surgery, his abdomen was distended, which in turn constricted his lung capacity. By the following morning, a week after the accident, it was obvious things were going in the wrong direction. Don's coloring was off, and he was barely breathing. The doctors warned me that unless his breathing improved, he might not survive.

I felt fragile, weak, and confused. I had honestly thought he was going to be fine and would recover over a period of time, probably two or three months. I had to fight to keep God's promise in front of me. It seemed as if everything was coming apart, and I was being dragged down into my own depression. I had never been that frightened and could find no sense of hope.

The darkness overwhelmed me.

Routinely I got up each morning, and one of my first tasks was to call the ICU nurses' desk. "What kind of night did my husband have? What was his blood pressure? His respiratory rate? What level of oxygen?"

Each time the nurses were helpful and kind.

Except once.

The ninth day Don was in the ICU, I called from my hotel room. It was about seven thirty in the morning, my usual time to call and ask how he had spent the night. When someone answered, I identified myself and started through my list of questions. I must have asked all of them without getting an answer, so I paused and waited.

"Oh, honey, you don't need to know those things," the nurse said. "You're only the wife."

I'm not a confrontational person and would normally ignore such stupid, petty comments. This time I was angry. I had asked normal and reasonable questions. On the previous mornings I had had no problems.

Something snapped inside me, but I kept my voice calm and said, "Let me speak to your supervisor."

"Just a minute, please."

From the tone of her response, it seemed obvious that she had no idea I was upset by her statement. I drummed my fingernails for a few seconds, trying to calm myself down.

The new voice identified herself as the head nurse. I explained who I was and what the other nurse had said to me. The woman listened to my entire explanation and said, "I'm so sorry that happened."

I said nothing, but waited.

"Please hold on and I'll get his chart," she said. Within seconds she was back on the line and answered my questions.

I never had a problem again when I called.

11.
"He's Given Up"

After his surgery Don went into a state of depression and wouldn't breathe deeply. Doctors said he had double pneumonia. Each day he became weaker and weaker.

This is difficult to write about even now. Don simply gave up and didn't want to live. I didn't realize the effect of intense, unstoppable pain, not to mention the surgeries and medications and how they affected him. Even if I had thought about the cumulative effects, it wouldn't have made any difference.

I didn't want my husband to die.

God, he doesn't want to live. Please, please make him want to survive.

I yelled at Don—it's not something I'd done often, but I yelled. I pleaded and I cried. But no matter what I said, my words seemed to make no difference. Don wouldn't talk to me. He remained nonresponsive except for turning his head away from me. Most of the time he'd stare at the ceiling of the ICU pod.

"You have to get well!" I implored him. I reasoned with him. I tried to talk softly. I quoted Bible verses and reminded him that people were praying for him.

It didn't matter. Nothing changed.

As he lay there, I thought, *So you want to give up now. You went*

*through a horrible, horrible accident, but you survived. Now you want to
give up! What is wrong with you?*

At one point I was worn-out and desperate. "You're not happy
to be back with me and with our three kids, are you? You just want
us to suffer! How could you be so cold and uncaring about me, and
especially about the kids? What's wrong with you?"

I stopped, ashamed of myself for what I'd yelled. I felt a great
sense of guilt because I was his wife. I loved him and had borne him
three children. I should have been able to reach him. If anyone could
connect with him, why shouldn't it be me, his wife?

A few times during those days, I wondered what life would be
like without Don. He was only thirty-eight and had always been the
head of our family. He had never, ever been afraid of anything or
hesitant to try a new adventure.

He'd been the one who wanted to do the bungee jumping or sky-
diving. He couldn't swim, and yet he'd get on the lake with the teens
and try to water-ski. He was the man who could face any challenge.
This was the man who knew no fear, and there wasn't anything he
couldn't overcome or couldn't do if he tried.

I stared at him and my body shook. He wasn't helping himself,
and I didn't know what more to do. This wasn't the Don to whom
I had been married for fifteen years. I wanted to shake him and
scream—anything to make him want to live.

Nothing I said changed him. I didn't understand that he was
depressed, and no one explained to me the effects of his medications.
I saw only the results and didn't understand the cause.

You're just stubborn.

And Don could be stubborn. I would tell myself that he was mad
about the fact that he was injured so badly, and he didn't want to
breathe deeply. I told myself anything to explain why he wouldn't
even try—and that lack of trying kept me upset.

"Don has given up," I said to those around me. "He doesn't want
to live."

That much was true, and even the doctors told me that if he didn't fight, he wouldn't make it.

God, how do I reach him? I don't know how to cope or what to do.

He was worn out by the pain, and fighting to survive had destroyed all his reserves. He later told me he had begged God to take him so he wouldn't have to hurt so much. He couldn't tell me or anyone those things at the time. If he had said something as simple as, "I want to die so I can go to heaven," I would probably have been even more upset.

I stopped yelling at him and went through a long time of prayer. Don had lived through the accident. Was that all God meant when he spoke to me? That he would survive a horrendous crash and die less than two weeks later? If Don was going to be all right, something had to change. *Don had to change.*

What should I do? What should I do?

———

To make everything worse, Dr. Bruce Houchins met me one evening after I left the ICU pod. While Dr. Greider had given me a sense of peace and comfort, Dr. Houchins had the opposite effect. He had a brusque manner that made me want to disappear before he could see me. That day he caught me as I came out of Don's pod.

Dr. Houchins was the head of the trauma team, and he visited Don several times a day. Despite not having a winning bedside personality, he seemed determined not to lose Don. I saw him at his worst and at his best.

He often talked to Don for several minutes in clear, demanding tones. His manner was sometimes offensive, but I appreciated that he didn't try to give me false encouragement.

That same day I had overheard two doctors outside Don's pod. I didn't catch everything they said, but enough to understand they were talking about putting Don on a ventilator. It was clear he was in grave danger. Nurses came in every four hours to administer breathing treatments and tried their best to help him. To attempt to strengthen Don's lungs, a nurse placed a plastic mouthpiece into his mouth and asked him to breathe out; the force would push a ball up inside a clear container. Nurses told me that even that device wouldn't do much good unless Don breathed.

"Breathe! Breathe!" the nurses would say.

"Hurts."

That was the only response I heard from him.

That evening, Dr. Houchins met me out in the hallway. Don had been delirious a few times, and I knew the situation was acute.

"He refuses to breathe. If he doesn't, he'll die." He turned and walked away.

Tears slid down my face. I didn't know what to do or say. I prayed silently and fervently, but I wasn't sure right then that God was listening.

Some of my most vivid memories of the next few days were of having to look at Don, urging him, pleading with him to try to breathe. They had him hooked up to a machine, and he was supposed to blow into it to clear out his lungs. He couldn't do it, and there was little breath. He was also in excruciating pain.

I look back now and realize that Don was depressed and worn-out. He didn't care or want to breathe more deeply.

"Breathe, Don!" I must have said those two words repeatedly. Several times a day the nursing staff urged him to try.

Because I wasn't aware of what was going on inside him, I became angry. "You're not trying!" I said.

Tears flowed down my cheeks.

He doesn't care. He doesn't want to survive.

"If he doesn't start breathing," Dr. Houchins told me the next time I saw him, "we'll have to put him on a ventilator." I knew that if they put him on a ventilator, it meant there was a good chance Don wouldn't survive.

I wasn't in the pod when Dr. Houchins yelled at Don, but Don told me about it months later. The doctor kept demanding, "Breathe! Breathe! You have to breathe."

"Can't."

"Then you're dead! You'll die if you don't breathe."

Don mumbled that it hurt too much.

"All right! Don't breathe! Just give up! You're dead. You're going to die if you don't breathe." He leaned down, almost in Don's face. "Can you get that into your mind?"

———

I needed help.

While I was praying for Don to try to breathe, I thought about David Gentiles. If there was anyone who could get through to my husband, David was the one. He was a pastor in the San Antonio area, which is about two hundred miles away.

I went back to my room and placed a call to David. I had accepted the truth that I wasn't going to be able to help Don on my own. To my relief, David answered almost immediately. I forced myself not to start crying. I explained about Don not wanting to live. "I don't know what to do. He's not going to make it unless something happens." Then the tears took over, and I couldn't say anything more.

David listened to everything and asked a few questions before he said, "I'll leave right now. I should be there in about three hours."

After I hung up nothing had changed, but I felt better. David was Don's best friend and the only other person in the world who could get right in Don's face and make him listen.

True to his word, David arrived about three hours later. Looking up from my seat in the ICU waiting room, I saw him walking quickly toward me. David had curly brown hair and always wore a moustache. He wasn't a tall man. In fact, he was shorter than me, about five foot four. But his eyes caught people's attention. They could draw people in. When David looked at others, they could see he really cared about them, deeply cared. His were the type of eyes I can see Jesus having—eyes that look into my soul and feel my joys, my hurts, and my pain.

We talked in the hallway for a few minutes. David hugged me, and his love for both of us strengthened me again. Even though it was late at night, since David was a minister, the staff said he could see Don for ten minutes.

After David went into the pod, I sat in the waiting room and prayed that those ten minutes would be enough for a change in Don.

When David came out of the ICU, he told me Don had said, "I don't have it in me, I can't make this. I've run out of gas."

"You have to make it. You've made it this far—" David had argued.

"I don't know if I want to make it."

"You have to make it. If not for yourself, then for the family."

"I can't make it—"

"We'll pray you through this," David had told him. "We'll pray for you to want to make it. We won't let you go!" Then he'd prayed fervently for his friend.

I can say this much: David stayed in my husband's room for only the allotted ten minutes, but it was enough.

By the time our friend walked out of the pod, Don was a different man. He had a new resolve—a determination about him—something that hadn't been there since the accident.

That night I had more peace than I'd experienced anytime since I first arrived at Hermann.

Don wants to live. We're over the worst.

By the next day the pneumonia was better. As Don often says, "Our friends prayed it away." More important, he really wanted to survive. He began to earnestly try to breathe.

As Don himself told me, he hadn't wanted to live anymore, but something changed him after David's visit. He's convinced God gave him the will to live.

He breathed on his own. It wasn't deep, but it was much stronger and deeper that it had been.

Don's inability to breathe—which I didn't understand—was probably my lowest moment in his recovery. No one suggested he was depressed, and I didn't realize that he was in such pain that he couldn't have done much for himself.

12.

THE FIXATOR

We were over the worst. At least that's what I thought. Don was still in the ICU, but he was making an attempt to live. His dying of pneumonia truly was the worst circumstance I faced at that time.

Or was I wrong?

On the twelfth day after the accident, a newer, serious problem became evident. No one had said anything more about the missing femur. I'm now aware that until they knew Don would live, it wasn't significant for them to consider the options.

Dr. Greider sat down with me and talked about Don's progress. "And now, Eva, you have to make a serious decision. I'm sorry, but you must do it rather quickly. Don's lungs have improved, but we can't give him the extensive breathing treatments he needs in his current condition."

I don't remember most of the conversation, but he talked about the eleven-hour surgery they had done the night Don arrived at the Hermann Trauma Center. On that night they had completed what needed to be done to allow him to survive until future treatment.

"We have to elevate him to do the type of breathing treatments he needs, and we can't do it with the left leg the way it is. So we have two choices. We can amputate his leg, or we can try the Ilizarov apparatus." Dr. Greider explained to me what he also called a *fixator*. I had seen people with metal halos on their heads for neck and back injuries, so I had some idea of what it would look like.

I later learned that doctors normally insist that candidates undergo months of counseling before they allow the Ilizarov frame to be used on them. In Don's case there wasn't time for counseling. The Ilizarov frame couldn't replace the missing bone, but if successful—and that was a strong *if*—the device would stretch the bones by pulling from both ends. With the Ilizarov method a new bone is created after the old bone is intentionally broken above and below the original breaks. The original broken ends are pushed closer and closer together, building a new bone. In Don's case, if successful, the broken pieces would eventually meet and form a new femur.

"We can give you no guarantee that it will work," Dr. Greider said. "Besides that, it's extremely painful. The emotional and psychological distresses are overwhelming. Also, it's never been tried on a femur before."

He gazed intently at me, I assume to gauge my response. I nodded that I understood.

"He'll have to live with that heavy frame on his leg for months to recover, and during that time he will never have one day without pain. A great deal of pain."

"Months?"

"Perhaps years." And he said again, "It's extremely painful."

I tried to follow his words and nodded a few more times. His next statement shocked me even more.

"Even after going through all of this, your husband might still lose his leg."

While I tried to make a decision, he explained that if they amputated the leg, they would fit him with a prosthesis, and Don would learn to walk with it.

He didn't push me to make a decision right then, although he said we needed to move as quickly as possible. With his leg in traction, Don's lungs could not be completely cleared with the necessary breathing treatments. He would continue to be at risk for pneumonia, which could be fatal. I wished it were a decision Don could make, but I knew I had to decide.

Here it is again. Another decision and another push out of my comfortable lifestyle where my husband made the major choices.

No matter what choice I made, the result would be painful for Don. He loved to walk, and he enjoyed tennis, bike riding, and snow skiing. A prosthesis didn't seem right to me. I could think only of the consequences of his losing his left leg. It was difficult to make that choice for him. Neither one seemed like a good option.

I had to weigh inside my head what I thought Don would be the happiest with in the end. I tried to think of his reaction, and I felt that if there was any chance to save his leg, that's what we needed to do. The Ilizarov offered that chance.

For a minute or two, I sat quietly and prayed silently for guidance. I wanted what was best for my husband. I would have liked to spend a few days seeking the Lord's will, but we didn't have a few days. At most, I had minutes.

I didn't hear any audible direction from God, but in my heart, I knew what I had to say: "Use the device."

"It is extremely painful, and it takes months to recover," the doctor repeated. He wanted me to make the decision, and it was clear he didn't want to influence my choice. He added, "But if we don't use the Ilizarov frame, we'll have no choice but to amputate."

"I'll sign the consent form."

In saying those words, I knew I had made the right decision. No matter how much Don suffered—and it would be far more than I could have imagined—I still believed I had done the right thing. I signed the form.

Dr. Greider told me that since the procedure had never been

used on a femur, the hospital would have to order parts for the frame because they weren't available at Hermann. He explained his plan to install the device as soon as they arrived, which would probably be the next day.

Don underwent a twelve-hour surgery to attach the fixator on his left leg. I sat in a different waiting area. A few friends dropped by early in the morning, but after about two hours, I was by myself.

It was the first time I had faced a surgery with no one else present. Another unusual factor was that I was the only one in that particular waiting area. At first I felt a sense of loneliness, but then something happened. As I sat there, looking out the windows at downtown Houston, I felt God's comfort.

Over the past two weeks, there had been little time to sit quietly. People always seemed to be around, or the medical staff was pressing me to make decisions. Something constantly needed my attention.

Dr. Greider had alerted me that the surgery would take several hours, so I had plenty of time to sit and unwind. It was a blessed respite for me. Alone in that room I could sit quietly and let God's peace wash over me.

I didn't know then that it would be a long time before I would have the chance to do that again. While Don was in surgery, having his leg steadied with wires and rods, God was steadying my soul with words of peace and comfort. I thought of Jeremiah 29:11, "'For I know the plans I have for you,' says the LORD, 'They are plans for good and not for disaster, to give you a future and a hope.'"

Those words reminded me once again that I had heard God's promise and everything was going to be all right.

Hours later, when Dr. Greider came to tell me Don was out of surgery, I had a stronger spirit of peace. I was ready to take the next step.

Later they put a second fixator on his left arm. Six rods went through the top of his arm and onto the bone. Dr. Greider placed large, stainless steel bars above and below Don's arm to stabilize it. The forearm bones had been shattered.

The rods were about the size of a pencil. As I understood, the procedure allowed Dr. Greider to take bone fragments from Don's right pelvis and place them in his left forearm. "This is like taking core samples," he said, "when they drill for oil wells."

A plastic surgeon removed thirty-two square inches of skin from Don's upper right thigh to place over the huge wound in his left arm. Then they embedded a Teflon strip between the newly placed bones in his forearm to prevent them from growing and attaching to each other. As we later learned, the Teflon technique didn't work quite right on the arm. Despite the precautions taken, the bones healed, but they attached themselves to each other.

Since the initial surgery, Don has had no pronation or supination in his left arm. That's the fancy way of saying that he can't straighten out his arm at the elbow, and he can't turn his palm down or up.

"I'm always ready to shake hands," Don once said, because that's the way his hand is.

The arm fixator weighed approximately twenty pounds, about ten pounds less than the one on his left leg.

On February 1, following the surgery on Don's left leg, hospital staff moved him into a regular room in Hermann with big windows. When they brought Don into the room, I had to fight to hold back my tears. Strangely, they weren't tears of sadness or even horror. On his left leg was a heavy, massive steel halo that went from his hip to below the knee. I didn't think of it as horrific. I saw it as the device that would give Don a chance to keep his leg. I've never been squeamish about anything other than vomiting, so seeing the device didn't bother me.

At that time, of course, I had no idea of the pain and suffering Don would endure while the device worked on his leg. I didn't know those wires would be pulled through his leg muscles as the bone was slowly regrown and would leave permanent scars down his thigh.

I saw it as a medical miracle, something that was moving us back toward normal.

I thanked God for bringing Don through the surgery, and then I relaxed. I'm glad I didn't know then how long and how painful getting back to normal was going to be. My first impression would change and evolve as time passed. Regardless, I was always able to see the Ilizarov apparatus as a device to save the leg. For that I was grateful, but I would grow to despise the pain it caused Don. At times it was difficult to separate my two emotions.

When Don woke after surgery, he was horrified at what he saw, and the pain was even more intense than before.

"What is this? Do those wires go all the way through my leg?" he screamed.

I explained about talking to Dr. Greider. I was factual and cool. "It's a bone-growth device. They call it a fixator."

Originally it had been developed to help those with the congenital condition where one leg was shorter than the other. But researchers learned that the body could form new bones between gaps in response to the mechanical force of the Ilizarov frame. Despite excruciating pain, the frame stretched the bone.

At the break in Don's left leg, OR staff had inserted what looked like piano wires right through the bone. They anchored the femur Ilizarov apparatus in the hip with rods, each about the circumference of a pencil. Dr. Greider drilled holes for four rods that went from Don's groin to the side of his left hip.

Thirty-two wires went completely through the bones in Don's leg and out the other side. Those wires were attached to four metal halos separated by rods that ran horizontal to his leg. It looked like a futuristic torture device.

Every four hours a nurse came into the room and turned the screws slightly to stretch the bones. The thirty-two pinholes had to be cleaned once a day. In time I would learn to clean the pinholes and turn the screws on my own. It was gut-wrenching to watch the pain it put Don in, but I felt a part of his recovery. It hurt me each time I saw his face grimace in pain.

———

I had had no idea what a monstrous device the Ilizarov frame was. I suppose I had assumed the screws were under the skin and not through the bones. I envisioned an external device that would act as an exoskeleton while the bone regrew. Until I saw it, I hadn't realized that those wires went completely through his leg and were embedded in his bone. Coming from a personal experience with knee surgeries and how painful they are, it was a horrible thing to see.

I knew we would be seeing that atrocious, stainless-steel frame for months.

I tried not to stare at the fixator as I added an explanation for Don. "Dr. Greider says it's the only chance to save your leg. It's a new technique. I'm not sure, but I think you're the first patient in this country to have such a device—at least you're the first one at Hermann Trauma Center."

He didn't respond, so I stared into his green eyes and said, "I believe it's worth the risk."

He said nothing, but I could tell he wasn't happy over my decision, and I had sensed he wouldn't be. Had the roles been reversed, I would have felt the same way.

He blinked and turned away from me.

To this day I'm convinced I made the right decision. My husband didn't like it. There were multiple times during the period after the frame was put on when he was angry with me. Some of his angry feelings were because of the excruciating pain. He had to wear that fixator for almost a full year.

Hardest of all was the fact that no one could assure us this device was going to work. I'm sure Don felt like a guinea pig in some mad-scientist experiment. I took on the role of constant encourager, which wasn't always easy. That task required additional energy from me, and my supply was already running low.

"Why did you let them do this to me?" he asked more than once. "If you had let them cut my leg off, I'd have been out of here by now."

I didn't try to justify my decision except to remind him, "I had to make the choice by myself. You weren't able to choose." I often said those words with tears in my eyes because I wanted him to understand I had tried to do the best thing for him.

"I could have had a prosthesis and I would have been fine. Why did you do this to me?"

Although I was aware that he grumbled at me because of his pain, it still hurt. This wasn't the man to whom I had been married for fifteen years.

Despite my understanding his pain, my tears flowed. I had only one answer, and I said it in several ways: "I thought I was doing the best thing for you."

———

The new room in Hermann was larger, and I was able to stay with Don all day and night. The staff gave him a nice corner room in the tower building with large windows looking out over Rice University.

In the airy room I felt I had a base and a place to stay. I didn't want to leave. To write about it makes it sound illogical (and it is), but as long as I remained inside the room, I could monitor Don's condition, even though I couldn't do anything to make him better. And yet no matter how low I felt, I didn't consider leaving the hospital.

I don't know how many times visitors urged me to take a break or to go for a walk out in the fresh air. "Go to the cafeteria and get something to eat." "Why don't you go home for the night and come back in the morning?" "Give yourself a break and get your hair done."

They meant well, and I appreciated the concern and kindness, but it was too difficult to leave, even for twenty minutes for a meal.

It took me a long time to admit it to myself, but something deep inside me felt that if I left the room, Don wouldn't make it.

While we were in that room, we had the same nurse every day. His name was Ibraham. He was from India and spoke with a soft accent. He was of average height, with dark, close-cropped hair. He was a wonderful man, and there was no doubt he cared deeply for his patients—not only their physical needs but their emotional needs as well.

Besides that obvious compassion, I appreciated that he didn't talk down to me or feel I didn't need information. Whenever I asked a question, Ibraham carefully explained what he was doing for Don, as well as the reason for it. He was always so careful with Don's legs and arms. He often apologized when Don would wince from pain.

Ibraham was also quick to encourage if he noticed the slightest improvement, especially in Don's breathing. The room was cheerful, and Ibraham's presence was a calming influence.

I wish it could have remained that way.

13.

THE HELP I DIDN'T
KNOW I NEEDED

While he was still in the ICU, Don had developed pneumonia, and the staff had to give him breathing treatments as best they could. With the Ilizarov apparatus in place, the respiratory therapist could begin more rigorous breathing treatments.

The first time I witnessed it, I was shocked.

A nurse came into the room, and she raised him to a sitting position. Using her hand, she thumped him on the back and chest. *Thumped* may be a mild way of saying it—Don said they beat on his chest. Even though it was something that had to be done, as a witness, it seemed awfully painful. The nurses were doing the right thing for him because the beating loosened the mucus. The respiratory therapist explained that the beating had to be done in a certain way to be most effective. She smiled and said, "It sounds worse than it really is." Even to this day, I'm sure she would get a strong argument from Don.

The thumping helped, but the medical staff also brought in what I call a "smoking device." The official name is *nebulizer*. They connected it to the oxygen valve, filled it with albuterol, and then had Don inhale the vapor. It helped him breathe and prevented fluid from building up in his lungs.

After Don was moved into the regular room, a group from the church came to visit Don and to see me. There were two couples a little older than Don and me, along with another woman. One of the couples had taken us to dinner at an exclusive restaurant a few months earlier.

At that time, I had sat in the back of their Suburban, thinking, *I can't believe this is happening.* It was the type of restaurant Don and I could only dream of going to. It had been a wonderful evening with good company in an amazing place. We had not really visited with the couple, except when we passed each other at church.

After only minutes of visiting, one of them said to me, "We're taking you to dinner."

"We're serious," another said with a smile. "You are leaving now, or we'll grab you and force you to leave."

Before I could protest and decline with appreciation, one woman said, "We've brought someone [whose name I can no longer remember], and she's going to sit with Don. If you're needed, she'll call—"

"I'm not hungry—"

"We're going to eat at Rice Village," she said, as if I hadn't interrupted her. Located near Rice University since the 1930s, Rice Village is a delightful shopping center in Houston and has dozens of restaurants in its sixteen-block area. I still didn't want to leave.

Even I was aware that it was an emotional response and not a logical one. Many women in long-term care situations become prisoners in their homes or in the hospital. I was one of them. We're not superstitious, but it's as if fear of what might happen while we're gone keeps us in emotional chains.

"That's kind of you and thoughtful, but how can I enjoy going out when Don is here?"

"He's going to be fine without you for forty-five minutes."

I tend to be a people pleaser, and I don't confront people easily. I sensed that if I protested, my friends would lovingly gang up on me and dismiss every argument.

It was easier to say yes. "Thank you."

They assured me that the woman who was staying would handle everything and call the restaurant if anything changed.

The two women and I walked to the front of the hospital while the men went to get the car. It was a nice day in Houston even though it was early February. The sun was shining, and it was just cool enough to warrant a light sweater. I climbed into the back of the same Suburban. Even though the ride lasted no more than fifteen minutes, I was constantly thinking about how Don was doing.

I remember two significant things about that outing. First, it was at a cafeteria in Rice Village. There were several food choices, and making more choices was not something I wanted to do, but I stumbled through the line with my friends. Once I was seated with those kind people around me, I relaxed. For perhaps half an hour I was able to push away any thoughts of responsibility or obligation.

Second, it was the best food I'd tasted in years. Or perhaps it wasn't that good, but I was that hungry. I had eaten very little since the accident. Even when I went to the hospital cafeteria, I gobbled my meals, hardly tasting what was on my plate.

I've since learned that other caregivers respond the same way and either ignore meals or eat little. Some go the other way, probably from stress and anxiety, and scarf down immense quantities. Either way, they hardly taste what they consume.

I made a promise to myself that evening. I was going to follow the example those dear friends from the church set for me. After this was over, if I heard someone was in a long-term caregiving situation, I'd remind myself that the caregiver needed relief, even if only for thirty minutes. The best way to provide that break was to do what my friends did. Show up and say, "I'm taking you to . . ." and insist on the other person leaving, and accepting no argument while making certain that a trustworthy person remains with the patient so the caregiver won't have to worry.

The church people were wonderful. They knew what I needed even if I didn't want to leave my self-imposed isolation. Again, that's typical of those of us in long-term-care situations. We are so caught up in our loved one's care, we tend to forget about ourselves.

14.

A SHOCKING TRUTH

Don was out of the ICU and in a large corner room, but he still struggled with breathing. One day Dick and Anita Onarecker came in and visited for a few minutes; then Dick asked if he could talk to me in the hall. He first expressed his joy that Don was alive and making some improvements; then he took my hand. I must have looked shocked because Dick asked if I had heard the details from the wreck.

All I knew was that Don had been hit by a Department of Corrections truck. Dick told me that he and Anita had come up on the accident. After waiting a long time, he had walked up to an officer on duty to ask if he could pray for anyone.

I gasped when I heard his next words.

"Everyone in the wreck is fine," the police offer said, "but the man in the red car is dead."

That was the first time I'd heard that Don had been a fatality. I knew he had been critically injured, but not that he had actually died.

Dick told me he had gotten into the car to pray for Don. He prayed, then sang, and then prayed again. "When I sang, 'What a Friend We Have in Jesus,' Don started singing with me."

When Don joined him in the hymn Dick scrambled back out of the wrecked car and shouted, "He's alive!"

At that moment it wasn't the fact that Don had died or that Dick had begun to sing with him that captured my attention. It was the hymn itself. Ever since I was a child, I had heard the story of how that hymn had been my Grandma Pentecost's favorite. She had asked that it be sung after a tragedy in their town because she truly believed we should bring everything to God in prayer.

When I heard that was the song in Don's mouth after Dick prayed for him, I knew again that God was letting me know his hand was on my husband. And God was in control.

During the many days that followed, that song would come to mind repeatedly. It was as if God had sent me a special message to reaffirm his presence.

15.

ANOTHER PROBLEM

Don stayed in the lovely corner room with windows at Hermann Memorial Hospital for slightly more than a week. We had a nice view of the city of Houston. It seemed like a very special room, especially after the ICU and waiting rooms. I hoped the new location and being able to see outside would improve Don's spirits after having been in the windowless ICU for two weeks.

I continually looked for ways to bring some joy into his life—something to make him smile. For a few nights I was able to watch the fireworks from the large windows above the Astrodome. For a few minutes I was transported away from the drudgery of the hospital to delight in the bursts of color over Houston.

But it didn't last.

On February 9, a clerk from the personnel department came to the room and said, "We're going to be moving Mr. Piper to St. Luke's tomorrow." St. Luke's Episcopal Hospital is in the same Texas Medical Center but not part of the Hermann Trauma Center.

"Why?" I asked. "Why do we have to move?"

"Your insurance won't continue if Mr. Piper remains here. Hermann Memorial is not part of your insurance plan."

"But the ambulance brought—"

"They brought him here because of the trauma, *and* it was a medical emergency. Now that he's stable, we have to move him to where your insurance will cover the costs."

Obviously, the staff person upset me, but he was only the messenger. As calmly as possible I asked, "Where do I go or who do I see to stop this move?"

"To the administrator's office. It's on the first floor."

I didn't hesitate to see the administrator. Taking that step was a big stretch outside my level of comfort, but this was about Don and his getting well. I was determined to go as far out of my ease as I needed.

The hospital administrator was kind and agreed with me that it would be better if Don stayed. "But it's out of my hands," she said.

"Is there nothing you can do?"

"I've done everything I know to prevent this from happening, but I can't stop it."

"Surely there is some way—"

"Nothing," she said, "unless you come up with the funds to keep him here."

"That isn't possible," I said.

I tried a few more times, but she was adamant—kind but unwavering.

I thanked her and left with a heavy heart. After I went back to the room, I thought of something Chris had said when he was in first grade. All five of us were in the car. It happened at a time when a special brand of tennis shoes had come on the market. He wanted a pair very badly, but they sold for about a hundred dollars.

"We're not going to buy them for you. They cost too much."

He sat in the back seat quietly for a minute or two, and then he said to his twin brother, "My mom's a teacher and my dad works for God. We're never going to have any money."

I smiled as I continued walking to the elevator. That memory did lighten my mood.

I understood the situation with the hospital. Our finances were tight, and I believed the administrator did try to keep Don at Hermann. Back inside the room I called our lawyer and explained what happened.

He called me back about twenty minutes later. "I'm sorry. I tried, but the administrator is right. I couldn't budge her."

I suppose part of my being upset was the matter of my comfort level again—my own comfort. At Hermann, I could find the parking garage, knew the location of vending machines, and had no trouble getting to the cafeteria. More important, I had become acquainted with most of the staff on all shifts and had grown comfortable with them—especially Ibraham, who had been so involved in Don's recovery. I felt they were giving Don the best possible human care.

With all the ups and downs with Don's problems, each minor change seemed enormous. I wanted things to stay calm. "I don't need any additional disruptions," I said to myself.

It sounds silly perhaps, but I had been born at Hermann Hospital and had never been to St. Luke's, so I felt I had a connection where we were. The real problem, which I accepted only in retrospect, is that I didn't want to deal with anything new.

Despite that, I was able to say, "Okay, there's nothing I can do to change things. I don't like it, but that's what we need to do."

I was upset and was aware of how I felt. My immediate task was to accept reality, relax, and prepare for the change.

I went back to see the hospital administrator, secretly hoping something had changed. (It hadn't.) I asked, "How are we going to do this?"

"We'll move him by ambulance. You can drive your car and follow them. By the time your husband arrives at St. Luke's, he'll already have been checked in, so you may go directly to his room." She told me the room number as well.

Room 2115. I didn't know it at the time, but we would be in that room for weeks.

On February 9, 1989, less than a month after the accident, we moved to St. Luke's Episcopal Hospital, which is about five city blocks from Hermann.

Exactly as the administrator promised, Don was transported by ambulance, and I followed in my car. It was a painful experience for my husband, as I knew it would be. Just to move him out of the bed with the fixators on his leg and arm was a huge ordeal for Don and the attendants because they had to figure out how to do it. And each movement sent searing pain through his body. I stood there, trying not to cry out as I watched his face pale with each move.

Every time the ambulance slowed, he could feel it, along with every small bump in the road. All movements with that device on his leg and arm, even slight ones, shot pain throughout his body.

I had no trouble finding the parking garage, which was well marked. Once I got inside the hospital, I took the elevator to Don's room on the twenty-second floor. I walked into the room, and the shock hit me.

I wanted to cry.

The room was about half the size of the one at Hermann. That was disappointing but far from the worst aspect. The wallpaper was green with cream stripes and was peeling in the corner. That fact alone gave it an old, uncared-for feel. There was a window, but when I went to it, I could see only another building. The only other furniture consisted of an old, rust-colored Naugahyde recliner and a couch that was attached to the wall. A small TV hung on the wall. Across from the windows was the vanity area with a large wall mirror and sink.

With the massive device on Don's leg and his arm in the fixator, he needed a trapeze attached above the bed in order to sit up. This required an additional metal frame that increased the perimeter of the bed. To accommodate his bed, it had to be pushed almost completely up against that vanity area, leaving little room to move on that side. I felt as if I were cramped inside a cave.

This is depressing.

I'm not a difficult person to please. Part of my reaction may have been the drastic difference between the two rooms, but it was more than that. This was going to be Don's new home for weeks, possibly months. It was hardly the kind of room I would want anyone to convalesce in.

Don lay in bed, unaware of the room, and his pain was excruciating. He didn't have to say a word, and he didn't. He groaned a few times, but that was all. As he lay there, his head moved slightly backward and forward, which is what he did when in pain. They hadn't yet hooked up a pain pump.

As I stared at him, tears filled my eyes, I thought, *We went through all of that movement to this place and now he's gone backward.* I didn't know that for certain, because I was judging only from the amount of obvious pain he must have felt during the past hour.

I determined to put on a happy face for Don and for everyone else.

Before long—and as his watching wife, I was positive it wasn't quick enough—a nurse brought in a pain pump so Don could receive pain medication instantly when he needed it. I sighed in gratitude, knowing that was what he needed.

They moved Don on a Sunday, so I took personal leave on Monday. I simply couldn't leave his bedside until I knew he was responding to the medication.

Once Don was settled in on Sunday, I used the telephone in his room and started calling our friends and business associates so everyone would know our new home.

After a couple of hours, I thought about myself and tried to figure out how I would spend the night. At Hermann, the room had a large chair that opened up into a bed, and it was fairly comfortable. This room had a hard couch, and the back tilted down to form a bed—with a seam down the middle. I groaned to myself as I looked at it. After

I returned to work, that's where I would sleep Friday and Saturday nights as long as Don remained at St. Luke's.

As time went by, I brought my own pillow and blanket, along with a few personal items from home. It was comforting to have some of my own things close by. Along with the get-well cards that lined the windowsill, I put pictures of the kids.

Someone brought up a tape recorder so Don and I could enjoy listening to our favorite music. St. Luke's wasn't the Ritz Carlton, but it would be home for Don and me for the next several weeks.

———

Within a few hours after Don was moved, the hospital administrator from Hermann Memorial called me. "I have good news for you," she said. "Workers' compensation is going to pick up the cost of the room. We can move your husband back to Hermann if you want."

For a few seconds I thought about the situation. I didn't like the room where Don was, and it had been so much nicer at the other hospital. But it would mean moving him again in an ambulance.

"I appreciate it, but it's not worth it for Don." I told her how much pain the trip had caused. "I can't do that to him again."

16.

FINDING MY PLACE

During those days many prayers were lifted for Don, for me, and for our family. Almost every time I spoke with someone on the phone or friends came to visit, I'd hear, "I'm praying for you." I truly believed they meant it.

Those words brought great comfort to my heart, and I appreciated them all. Others went a step further and asked, "What do you need me to pray about?" or "Today I prayed that Don's pain would lessen . . . that Don would eat . . . that you would have a good night's rest."

Those people taught me the importance of specific prayers. Their petitions were more personal and more intimate. To me it showed additional attentiveness to our well-being.

I also took note of the consistent prayer warriors—those special individuals who continued to keep us in their prayers throughout Don's recovery. It didn't matter whether their prayers weren't answered immediately; they kept praying until they received answers, even though sometimes the answer was no.

I learned many lessons about prayer during those days. Our friends' prayers brought glimmers of pure light along my dark pathway.

In my blackest moments (and there were many), I reminded myself of God's promise that it would be all right. Some days I couldn't see how that was possible. I was able to keep my spirits up only because I clung to God's promises and felt fortified by the prayer of others. Our friends and family members supported me, and I'll always appreciate that. But at the worst times, my crying out to God was the one thing that kept me going.

I never questioned the choices I'd made about staying all that time in the hospital and about the Ilizarov apparatus that came later. Even though I had made those serious decisions, it didn't mean it was easy. Those days were truly a walk in the dark for me. So many times during Don's recovery—perhaps most of the time—I felt inadequate.

Most wives would probably have felt as I did. We are the ones who fix things and make the situations better and softer. There wasn't a thing I could do for Don except be there. I couldn't fix anything.

A few times I thought, *I can't keep going like this.* Before long I was fighting my own form of depression. Nothing would have stopped me from remaining at Don's side, and yet at the same time, I felt like a prisoner within my limited world.

It's not logical, but on an emotional level, I believed I had failed Don and everyone else. I kept thinking of things I *should* have been able to do. I was incapable of helping Don get better, especially when he was in deep pain. I was inadequate for not being able to care for our three children. It frustrated me that I couldn't go back to my classroom and teach my students. Although I was only away from my class for three weeks, it seemed as if I'd been gone much longer. I was convinced that every school day I missed, I failed my students.

"Oh, dear God, I don't know if I can keep doing this." Wasn't it my responsibility to keep up Don's spirits? Wasn't I, as his wife, the one who was supposed to make him better? I called it the Suzy Sunshine Syndrome (SSS), and I've since realized that many women experience such feelings.

No matter how low I felt or how inadequate, as soon as I opened the door to my husband's room, my bright smile had to be in place. "Hi, honey. How are you doing today?" During many of my visits, he was so depressed that he wouldn't acknowledge my presence. Though I didn't recognize the depression, the SSS had to function. I forced myself to make small talk—trying to keep everything pleasant and warm.

Each day it became more and more difficult to put on the Suzy Sunshine mask. I was giving everything I had each time I walked into the room, and I was getting nothing back.

Not one friendly word.

Not a greeting or even an occasional smile.

That went on day after day after day. I put so much of my energy into being a ray of sunshine, I was exhausted.

"Please, please, Lord, help me. I can't give up."

Not only was I trying to lift his spirits; I also had to perform and be Suzy for visitors. That added task of entertaining visitors took so much energy out of me—and later out of Don when he began to recover. Wasn't I obligated to smile constantly and encourage them so they wouldn't worry about Don? No one ever told me that was what I was supposed to do, but I believed I had to be up every moment for others.

But who's there for me?

In my worst moments that's how I felt; and yet there were those who cared. It was not so much the reality of being alone as it was the feelings of being stranded in the dark and not knowing which direction to turn.

Susan and Suzan, as well as my parents, did everything they could for me. My coworkers at school took over some of my responsibilities. Church members offered help. But when I was feeling crushed by the burdens I carried, I couldn't think about them. And yet in retrospect I don't know how I would have survived all those months without those loving, caring people.

I couldn't do anything to make Don better, and I couldn't lift my own spirits. So there were many, many dark days, long after the initial eleven-hour surgery . . . and the breathing problem . . . and the fixator installation on his leg. On my bad days it seemed as if I couldn't get myself together, and I was sinking slowly into a dark, bottomless pit.

17.

RETURN TO TEACHING

I didn't return to teaching until Don was moved to St. Luke's, which meant I missed almost three weeks of school. I went back to work for several reasons, but the most practical one was that our entire family relied on the insurance paid for by my school district. I hadn't accumulated many personal days, so I had no choice if I wanted to keep my job *and* our insurance.

I also truly needed to be with people outside the hospital. It would have been easier to stay in that room all the time and become like a hermit.

I did the best I could at school and believed I was able to do an adequate job. At the same time, teaching tore me up because I thought about Don while I was at school. I also thought about my kids and my students while I was at the hospital.

The church continued to pay Don's salary, but neither of us knew how long that would go on. One well-meaning friend from the church confided that there was some discussion concerning whether to continue paying it. I never tried to verify it, and the pastor, Barry, never said anything to Don or me.

True or not, it obviously concerned us. Others must have heard the rumor because one church member came to me and said, "You're not to worry. We're going to keep on paying Don's salary until he's out of this and back to work."

———

Ginny Foster, the pastor's wife, did many things for me. One of her kind actions that remains the most memorable was that she brought me snacks. My favorite snack was Cheese Nips and orange juice. I'm not sure how Ginny found out—perhaps she asked Nicole—but she brought me snacks regularly, especially during the early days when I wouldn't leave the hospital. It's funny how such a small thing can make such an impression.

During the days Don stayed in the ICU and even the first few days he was in a private room, I didn't leave the hospital, and that's when she was the most helpful. She went by our house and brought me fresh clothes, and she washed my dirty ones.

Ginny was never an overbearing presence, and she was there whenever I needed her. She was the liaison between what was going on outside the hospital and what was going on with Don. I'll always be grateful for her warm, sensitive nature.

Another thing: I don't have proof of this, but I am reasonably sure that she arranged for the people to come up and kidnap me and take me to dinner one night. That would have been so typical of her thoughtfulness.

———

I focused only on Don's surviving, especially the first few days, and didn't think about costs or insurance. Once he was past the question of survival, the hospital bills began to trouble me, and I became concerned about finances. I had no idea how much of the hospital bill my insurance would pay. I was smart enough to know that the figure would be astronomical.

Although I tried to live the one-day-at-a-time method and did it fairly well, once in a while my mind would focus on the bills and remember tragic stories I'd heard. I knew people who had exhausted their insurance and paid medical bills for years. I hoped we wouldn't be among them.

When I thought about the possibility of the church discontinuing Don's salary, I went into the protective-wife mode—as most women would. "How could they treat him like that? Where is their compassion? When the accident happened, Don was on his way to church, and there was never any evidence that it was his fault."

Don didn't hear my ravings. Those were mostly things I kept inside or said only when I was away from his room.

I was also angry because of the rumor. Don passionately served Jesus Christ. He put in more hours and effort than the church could afford to pay him for. Would they say he had become a liability? I now realize that in my fragile, emotional state, any rumor or negative voice was enough to throw my emotions onto the proverbial roller coaster. I did have serious moments of anger—especially when I felt anyone was mistreating my husband.

Of course, it all worked out, and there was no problem about the church continuing Don's salary. But for a long time, we didn't know. I also carried a little resentment that someone—anyone—would think of treating a minister that way.

That brings me to another powerful lesson I learned during those days. People say things because they assume the person wants or needs to know. I don't mean to question their motives, only their wisdom. By repeating rumors or making negative remarks, they inadvertently cause friction, misunderstanding, and anger. For a long time I felt someone hadn't wanted to treat Don fairly, even though that probably wasn't true.

My usual way to deal with those types of issues is to cry when I'm alone. I don't lash out or yell at people, and I don't try to hurt them by retaliating with angry or caustic words because I'm more of an internal person. Sometimes I simply go silent and can't talk. If I try, more tears come, so it's easier to go silent. In time I learned to wait until I'd calmed down before approaching someone and describing my feelings. Getting the problem out in the open was beneficial for everyone, especially me.

18.

"Thank You for Letting Me Minister to You"

Individuals from church or the school did many kind and loving things, and I want to point that out. However, many of them also said, "Please call us if you need anything."

I'm sure they meant those words, but that didn't help me. That offer doesn't help others who walk in the dark. If those of us in the dark don't know which way to turn or which voice to heed, we're not going to call anyone else. We simply stumble forward.

Those who did the most for me were the ones who simply acted without asking. Like Ginny, the most sensitive ones didn't wait for me to say anything. Once they discerned a need, they took over and did what they could.

I want to record one important thing because, even now, it remains powerful. It's about Stan.

Suzan kept close tabs on Don's progress. As a member of the youth council and a dear friend, she came up to the hospital frequently. Through Suzan, Stan learned that Don would hardly eat and that he was losing weight at what the doctor called "an alarming rate." Don had dropped at least 50 pounds, from a robust, six-foot-tall, healthy 210 all the way down to 150 pounds. The staff couldn't seem to stabilize him.

One time, only minutes before an orderly brought in Don's evening meal tray, Stan showed up, and later I assumed he had timed it that way. He's a big man, and to look at him you'd think he exemplifies the true macho type. Stan was dressed in his typical Alvin High School polo shirt with khaki pants. Although not huge, Stan still stood out in a crowd with his athletic build. While usually mild mannered, he could be very adamant when he felt strongly about something. After all, he was a football coach.

By then, Don was able to feed himself, but he simply didn't want to eat. That evening, the main course was chicken. He stared at it, ate a few bites, and turned his head away.

"You need to eat it," I said.

"Not hungry."

"You need to eat!" Stan ordered, as if he were talking to one of his football players.

Don shook his head.

"You're *going* to eat," Stan said. It was settled, and he wasn't going to let Don argue with him. "Open your mouth and I'll shovel it in."

To my surprise, Don obeyed and accepted a small piece of chicken, chewed it, and swallowed.

"Very good. Now the next bite."

Stan insisted on feeding him everything on the tray. After he'd finished, he looked at me with tears in his eyes, and said, "Thank you for letting me minister to Don."

That's when tears sprang into my own eyes.

For both Don and me, that experience was probably one of the single most loving gestures anyone did for Don during his entire hospital stay. I'm not sure why this memory stands out. Maybe it was because Stan put actions to his love for us.

The words of the hymn "They Will Know We Are Christians by Our Love" comes to mind. Many may think simply feeding Don chicken wasn't that big a deal. Yet I'll never forget the look on Stan's face when he finished feeding Don. You'd have thought he had just led his team to the state championship. He was proud and honored to be able to serve even in what I'm sure he thought was nothing difficult.

Stan's taking over and forcing Don to eat was yet another lesson I learned while walking in the dark. We tend to think we're a burden if we ask or allow someone to help. We fear we're an imposition; those who truly want to help see it as a privilege. I had to face that lesson repeatedly before I understood and joyfully allowed others to come to my aid and, even more, to accept it as an expression of their affection.

Don had more trouble accepting help than I did. He was the professional minister, the one who always comforted and encouraged others, and he did it well; however, he wasn't good at being on the receiving end. He got better at it, but for him it's still an ongoing struggle to allow others to give of themselves to him.

While Don remained the patient in the hospital, he and I were the learners.

Here's another important lesson I learned: It takes so little to affirm others' help and let them minister to us. Allowing friends to do even something simple, like make telephone calls or buy us a snack, required little from us, but their facial responses told us how grateful they were for being able to help.

Many times I thought, *That's the way the Bible wants us to behave.* Paul referred to the church as a human body on several occasions. He said that each member is important, and if one part hurts, the whole body suffers.

For more than a year, I saw the constant flow of the spiritual body of Jesus Christ trying to take away our pain.

19.

MY PRIVATE THERAPY

Don had been angry when I'd allowed the doctors to use the Ilizarov apparatus on his leg. Had I realized the excruciating pain he would endure every day, I might have consented to amputation. But it was done. I never believed I had made the wrong decision about the fixator. I just hated to see the torture Don was going through. I prayed for God to alleviate the pain.

It's too easy to say Don got used to the device. There was no way for him to get used to it because the pain was always there. Relentless. Agonizing. Thirty-two wires, each about the width of piano wire, went through his left leg. Four times every day a nurse turned the screws one millimeter. It was an extremely small turn but still enough to initially increase the pain each time. Later the pain subsided, but it never completely left. That procedure and the agony it caused left him exhausted.

After the fixators were on his leg and arm, visitors came into the room. Because of the huge, thirty-pound device on his leg, they gawked. I don't know what they expected or what they had heard, but few of them were able to focus on anything except the monstrous frame around Don's leg.

They usually asked the obvious question: "Does it hurt?"

To his credit, Don was gracious. "A little," was his frequent answer. He did feel a little pain, plus a lot more. He wasn't intentionally lying, and it was his way of taking care of his visitors. What good would it have done to describe the unremitting torture?

To my surprise, the worst responses to his device came from the big, tough-looking men. When they asked how the Ilizarov apparatus worked, I'd tell them about the pins going through the leg bone. Then they'd stare for several seconds at Don and at the frame. "I need to step outside a minute," they'd finally say. The device was just too gruesome for some male visitors to look at while they tried to talk to my husband.

I don't know if the men were wondering, *How would I feel with that thing on my leg?* or if they felt deep empathy for Don. I sensed that some of them focused on the apparatus and forgot about the man. That's easy to do when standing in a hospital room filled with unfamiliar machines and devices.

That's something else I learned from watching visitors. They made me determine that each time I visited a hospital room or a sickbed, I would keep the patient in focus.

Don was in extreme pain, and he didn't try to hide his agony, but he didn't want to talk about it either. The easiest way to do that was to minimize his condition in answer to visitors' questions.

———

As I think about how I handled everything, I've concluded that God gives people like me blinders when we go through such trials. Some situations are so painful we can't allow ourselves to focus on them again. We avoid these painful experiences by being unaware or unconscious of events around us. They're important, and we know they happened, but to dwell on them means to reexperience them.

Some events were so important while they were taking place

that I was sure I'd never forget. And yet, I haven't retained all of the details, though at the time I was sure every specific act would stay engraved in my memory. Over a period of time, some of those details became fuzzy. That may have been a self-protective response. Because so many things happened, I could hold on to only so much information.

As Don's wife I obviously remember certain things as more significant then he does. The pain and depression from which he suffered probably blotted out or obscured events for him that I focused on. I was at his side and struggled with deep emotional pain; he was in bed and fought physical and mental pain every minute.

One thing that helped was a call I received from Kenny Wood, whom we'd met during the summer of 1988, when he came as our youth camp pastor several months before the accident. At that time I was still adjusting to moving away from home and living in Texas. This was the first time in Don's ministry that I didn't have my parents around the corner to keep the kids while Don was busy with youth activities. By the time Don and I went to summer camp, I was having serious thoughts about whether I wanted to be a minister's wife.

Then in his early forties, Kenny was a little older than we were. He had an incredible gift of speaking to the heart, not only in his messages but in one-on-one conversations. Several times that week, Kenny and I walked the campus, and I felt comfortable talking to him. Kenny impressed me because he had a charming, natural way of talking to people. He helped me see my part in Don's ministry and why I was important. I learned later that he helped many others through the difficult phases of their lives.

About a week after the hospital staff moved Don into a room, Kenny called me. "How's Don doing?" he asked. I updated him on current information, and then he asked, "But how are you?"

"I'm fighting a few things. I have different feelings." I'm sure I said more than that. His question shocked me because visitors and callers rarely asked me how I was doing. They were concerned about

Don, which I expected, and they naturally focused on him. Because I didn't complain, I'm sure they assumed I was all right.

When Kenny called, I was all right in that I functioned. I did what I was supposed to do as Don's wife and the children's mother—or at least I tried. I doubt visitors had any indication of the turmoil inside my own heart. I don't blame them; I held back and hid my anguish.

"How *are you*?" he asked again.

I sensed it was more than a polite question and that Kenny really wanted to know.

"Not so good."

He said nothing but waited for me to talk, and I did. After I opened up and expressed my inner turmoil, we talked for a few minutes. Then he asked, "Do you journal?"

"I know *about* journaling," I said. "Several of my friends keep journals, but I've never done it."

"It might be a good idea for you to start," he said. "As you write, you can help yourself sort out what you feel and get your mind on the important issues."

Kenny went on to say that many times he wasn't sure how he felt about what was going on around him or what was churning inside him. "Without censoring myself and by writing freely in my journal, I learn to identify what's troubling me."

"I'm a fairly private person—"

"No one else has to see the journal, and you probably wouldn't want to show them. This is something *for you*—only for Eva—not for anyone else. You write from the heart, and it's just between you and the Lord, and he knows everything anyway."

I thought about what he said for a few seconds before I answered, "I think I could do that."

"Please do it."

"I'll try," I said, "but this is new to me."

Until then, I'd never considered journaling. However, my emotions were in such turmoil I was willing to do anything. I decided that it probably would be good for me while I sat across from Don in his hospital room.

I hadn't yet gone back to teaching at that time, but I still looked over papers my fellow teachers brought me at the hospital. After I finished I sat for a couple of hours each night with nothing to do, especially since Don still wasn't doing much talking.

I did exactly what Kenny suggested. At the gift shop, I bought a little tablet and started writing down the medical information. I started with basic facts, dates, types of surgery, people who came to visit, and those who sent flowers. I discovered that having a written record of those facts was helpful when new decisions or medical problems arose. I didn't have to search my tired brain for dates and procedures. Everything was written in my notebook.

After a few days I started including my perceptions and was open about my feelings. I reasoned that if I could write it down, I could figure out how to better understand myself and my situation.

I felt I had discovered my own private therapy.

I wrote almost every day during Don's recovery. As I continued to journal, I learned to focus on myself and tried to make sense out of the chaos. I definitely didn't do it to show anybody else, and I was determined that no one would ever read it (and they didn't).

More and more, journaling became my private therapy to sort out my feelings and enable me to get in touch with the way I viewed things. Just writing about unresolved issues was a big step toward resolving them.

I discovered that journaling helped my dark moods. In my journal I could write all the things I was feeling: the good and the bad, the pros and cons. It was a way to vent, to let me say the things I would never say aloud.

The writing allowed me to release my anger, frustrations, and fear. With my mind clear, I was able to decide if something was a situation I needed to address or one I needed to let go.

I wish I still had that journal. When Tropical Storm Allison roared through our part of the country in 2001, we lost my journal along with many other things.

———

One time, after I mentioned my private therapy, someone questioned me. "In your writing did you ever ask God why?"

At times I had questioned God, mainly, "Why did you let this happen to Don?" I knew that question was unanswerable, but sometimes in our emotional turmoil, we cry out for reasons or explanations.

Although at times I didn't like it, I accepted my role in caring for Don; I didn't feel any self-pity or ask God why I was put in the situation. However, I had a difficult time understanding why he would let something so awful happen to a man who was dedicated to serving him. It's that age-old question: Why do bad things happen to good people?

I became angry at times and yelled at God, "I'm tired! I can't keep doing this! I want my old life back!"

God accepted my anger, my frustration, and my questions. It was actually a relief for me to vent, and I felt stronger afterward. I became more sensitive to myself and also a little more aware of others' unspoken words.

Even today, when our adult children come into the room, I can tell immediately if something is bothering them. Without fail, I ask, "What's wrong?" Nothing they say can make me love them less. That's probably why they tend to confide in me: they're secure in my love for them.

Before the accident I was afraid to tell God how I really felt. I didn't want to disappoint him. Also, to pray about my true feelings meant being completely honest with God, and there were negative feelings I was ashamed of having.

During Don's recovery I realized I wasn't hiding anything from God. He already knew how I felt and why I felt that way. He was waiting for me to talk to him about my feelings as well as the problems.

Just like with my own children, there was nothing I could say that would make my heavenly Father love me less. So I opened up and, as they say, I let it all hang out. After my emotional tirades passed, I heard God's calming spirit telling me, "It's okay. I love you, and I'm here with you."

From time to time, I still journal but no longer do it daily as I did during those traumatic days. Nowadays, when I'm frustrated with something or not sure which way to turn, I write in my journal to force myself to clarify what's going on inside my own head and heart. Many times after writing, I realize things aren't as bad as they may have seemed, or I come to understand why I'm upset. My private therapy still works.

Another invaluable therapeutic aid that helped me make it through those long, silent hours was reading my Bible. Perhaps that sounds obvious because I'm a Christian and the Bible is *our* book. I wasn't a stranger to the book, but I hadn't put in much effort to absorb its messages.

Since childhood, I've read my Bible regularly. And like many readers of the Scriptures, I underlined with a highlighter or pen. During Don's time in the hospital, my reading became more intense, more than just gaining understanding of God and finding guidance on how to live. As I read, I sought verses that brought comfort and encouraged me in my dark hours.

I found many of them. Verses I had once skimmed over took on new meaning and brought me solace.

During the months of Don's recovery, I also kept a journal of Bible verses—special scriptures that turned on the lights when darkness invaded my world. I call them my flashlight verses. I copied them into one of those small, spiral-bound notebooks. As I copied the verses by hand, the words became stronger and more meaningful to me.

Later, when I wanted to read something to lift my spirits or I felt particularly vulnerable, I'd turn to my flashlight verses or flip through my Bible-verse journal and read until one or more of them brought sweet comfort to my soul.

As a teacher, I'm aware that students learn from different teaching styles. The more learning styles I could incorporate, the better chance I had of reaching all of them. Some were strictly visual learners, and for others the ear was their primary form of intake. Many children—perhaps most—also enhance their learning if they have to go through the physical act of writing information. I used the same method on myself.

For example, I copied the verses below and read them several times while Don was recovering.

- "Trust in the LORD with all your heart; do not depend on your own understanding. Seek his will in all you do, and he will show you which path to take." (Prov. 3:5–6)
- "You will keep in perfect peace all who trust in you, all whose thoughts are fixed on you!" (Isa. 26:3)
- "'For I know the plans I have for you,' says the LORD. 'They are plans for good and not for disaster, to give you a future and a hope.'" (Jer. 29:11)
- "Cast all your anxiety on him because he cares for you." (1 Peter 5:7 NIV)

In my dark moments I read and reread many of those verses because I needed the reassurance and constant support God promised. I especially found comfort in thinking of God's plans for us.

I've never felt God *caused* the accident, and Don and I have never blamed God for human error and failure. The verse that helps me see this most plainly is one to which so many of us turn. I learned it as a child because it was Grandmother Pentecost's favorite verse: "And we know that in all things God works for the good of those who love him, who have been called according to his purpose" (Rom. 8:28 NIV). That verse gave me an anchor to hold on to during the uncertainty of those dark days.

As I meditated on Romans 8:28, I had no idea what God was going to do with the mess we were in, but I knew that in ways we weren't able to comprehend at that point, God would use even the accident for our good and for his glory.

Even now, after all these years, I'm blessed and amazed by the many ways God has brought immeasurable good out of our chaos.

———

Earlier I wrote about the turning point for Don—the time David Gentiles prayed for him. My turning point came the morning I received that rude answer from the ICU nurse. ("Oh, honey, you don't need to know those things. You're only the wife.") At the time I wasn't aware, but that's when I stepped beyond my private comfort space—and would do it many more times in the months ahead.

During those early days I had to push to get what I needed. I learned to ask questions until I not only had answers but I understood the situation. If I didn't grasp the meaning or if staff spoke with medical jargon, I learned to say, "I'm not in the medical field. Can you explain that again?"

It worked. I got what I wanted.

People sometimes speak of feeling empowered, and perhaps that's what it was. I think of it more as being persistent. I didn't go into a rage or raise my voice. When I became aware of things that needed doing or I required information, I asked and stayed steadily at it until I received an acceptable response.

The brief encounter with the insensitive nurse taught me something. If it was important to me, and the person to whom I spoke wasn't able or didn't seem interested in helping me, there would always be a supervisor above that individual. Just asking for the supervisor was usually all it took to motivate the recalcitrant staffer to go into action.

The event itself is quite amazing because in the past, when problems came, I was the soft, easygoing one. Don handled the big issues. That changed after the accident. A new side of me came forward—one that I wasn't even aware was a part of me.

These days, my kids tease me. "If you want something done, let Mom handle it." For instance, if we have a problem with the phone company or the electric bill, the kids say, "Put Mom on the phone; she'll take care of it."

My dad used to quote the old saying, "You catch more flies with honey than with vinegar." He was right, and that reality was enforced many times during Don's recovery. When I needed something, I didn't yell or demand; I kept my voice calm and polite, but I *persisted*, and it paid off.

In my walk in the dark, that was a powerful lesson that kept me moving forward. I wasn't in the light yet, but I was making my way forward. I could remain nice and kind, and as long as I was firm and clear about what I wanted, people were generally willing to do what they could.

Even today, if anything fails to grant satisfaction, "I need to speak to your supervisor" are my immediate words and what I also call the magic formula for satisfactory results.

20.

MY LEARNING TIME

I rarely felt totally at ease during the days Don remained in the ICU and the first few weeks afterward. Suzan Mauldin and Susan Long were my confidants, and I could open up to them about anything, including my anxiety about finances. When life seemed to close in on me or I felt exhausted and didn't know what to do, I could talk to either of them. They didn't try to solve my problems—which they couldn't—but they listened. And they cared.

Two things stand out as important when I talk about my two friends. First, neither was judgmental. They listened, and not once did I ever feel rebuked or doubted.

Second, they didn't offer advice. At times when I tried to talk with people, they'd try to fix problems for me or solve my issues by offering advice or telling me what to do. Mostly Suzan and Susan listened. I don't remember either of them saying, "You need to . . ."

During my walk in the dark, I had to learn how to respond when others tried to comfort me. I accepted their compassionate gestures and intentions without necessarily following their directions. Previously I had been one of those who reached out to others, and because I didn't want to offend anyone, I allowed them to make my decisions for me at times.

I learned so much during that time.

Before the accident, when I would visit people in the hospital, I felt the need to encourage them: "Everything is going to be okay . . . God is with you . . . God never gives you more than you can handle." Often I'd share Bible verses.

Only after the accident did I realize that when a person has been sitting in a hospital room for days and days, what she really needs is a listening ear. Perhaps that sounds obvious, but visitors didn't do as much listening to me as I did listening to them.

"You don't have to do anything for me," I wanted to say. "You don't have to remind me of God's presence or find ways to buoy my spirits. You don't have to remind me of God's never-failing love. Your being present here with me is a wonderful gift."

————

Here's another lesson I learned: I'm sure they weren't aware of it, but a few people who came to comfort me actually depressed my spirits because they talked about *their* bad situations or the problems *they* faced. I understand those are significant issues when people hurt, and there is a need to talk, but having to listen to their traumatic stories made me feel as if they were diminishing my situation.

So here's another piece of advice for visitors: Don't complain, criticize, or act judgmentally. Why burden the caregiver with concerns or problems that they don't need to know about? Be sensitive to the fact that those sitting by the patient (or even the patient) have about as much as they can handle. Don't overwhelm them with your problems. They have more than enough of their own.

————

A few others seemed to know all the things I needed to do for Don or for myself. They had advice from their experience or from stories they'd heard. I'm sure they meant their words sincerely; however, in my mind I didn't feel anyone really understood Don's and my situation. I smiled because I didn't want to hurt their feelings.

There were also the people who acted as if Don weren't in the room and told me how bad he looked or how much pain he must be in. That was bad enough, but it was usually only the prelude. They would go on and on about the horrific details from the accident and how tragic everything was. Not only was that discouraging to me but Don didn't need to hear those things.

Whether he appeared to be sleeping or unconscious, people shouldn't have taken the chance that he might be able to hear them. I support the old saying "If you can't say something positive, don't say anything."

After that kind of thing happened several times, in self-defense I figured out a few techniques to use when people tried to give me answers that weren't appropriate or didn't feel right to me: First, I smiled and thanked them. Nothing else. If the person persisted, I said, "I appreciate your being concerned, and I'm sure God will help me figure it out." Saying that let me off the hook; I wasn't saying no, but I wasn't saying yes. And by telling them I would pray about their advice (which I did), they couldn't argue with seeking divine wisdom. Once I appealed to God—and I was sincere about that—they had no additional advice to offer.

Because of my experiences, I've since learned to do what I wished some would have done for me. I try to provide the listening ear. That's what troubled individuals need more than anything else. Let them tell me what they want (or don't want) me to do. I want to be there *for them*. It's not a time for me to impose my pain or problems on them.

I've watched my dad provide counsel to others, and he's good at doing it right. He listens intently so that those who speak realize he hears them. Dad never folds his arms across his chest but either stands or sits with his arms at his sides. Occasionally, and if it's appropriate, he'll put his hand on the other person's shoulder. He looks people straight in the eye and nods as they talk. He connects with them. He also waits until they are finished talking before he responds. Often his response is in the form of a question, one that allows the speaker to elaborate the point or problem.

In my entire life, I've never heard my dad raise his voice or use a derogatory tone. He can make anyone he talks to feel as if he or she is the most important individual at that moment. Dad gives people his full, undivided attention. So often I've seen and experienced his ability to help them come to a decision on their own through his careful listening and questioning.

If someone is giving him advice, he uses a different tactic. He thanks the person and makes him feel appreciated for offering help. He doesn't promise to do anything.

As I watched Dad through the years, I realized he understood an important principle. When people offer suggestions, it's important for them to feel heard. Even if their advice is useless, they still need to know they've been listened to, and that's a way of affirming them. Dad does that well.

———

Most of the hospital staff were wonderful, and I want to make that clear. But there were exceptions. I've previously mentioned Dr. Bruce Houchins. He has since passed away, but he and Dr. "Red" Duke were the two trauma doctors at Hermann Memorial Medical Center. Dr. Duke is an icon in the Houston medical community, with his long, red handlebar mustache and slow, Texas drawl. Dr. Duke served as chief of trauma at Hermann. Whichever man was on duty when a patient came to the trauma center was the doctor who would handle that case.

Dr. Houchins took our case. He was one of those whom most would say had no bedside manner. He was irritatingly direct, pushy, and arrogant. My biggest complaint was that he didn't like to answer questions, even brief ones with answers that would have given me greater peace of mind. I wasn't sure if he felt my questions weren't worth his time or, like that rude nurse, he didn't think I needed to know because I was *only* the patient's wife.

His mean-spirited demeanor wasn't limited to his patients or to family members. He could be just as rude and condescending with the nurses.

Once I mentioned Dr. Houchins's poor bedside manner to one of Don's nurses. She stopped for a moment and nodded. Then she smiled and said, "That may be true. But if I or one of my loved ones were brought into this trauma center, I'd want him as my doctor. He never quits trying to save his patients."

As I continued to stay around the hospital, I began to understand what she meant. He *was* all the negative things I've said before, but he was also the man who refused to stop trying to help his patients recover. I firmly believe that without Dr. Houchins's unrelenting care, Don wouldn't have survived.

From that, I also learned another invaluable lesson. God uses difficult people and demanding situations to bring us to where God wants us to be. I like being the stronger person I've become. I wouldn't have turned out like this if it hadn't been for the uncooperative nurse, Dr. Houchins's harshness, and encounters with a few abrasive others. All those situations helped move me toward becoming more assertive and insisting on my personal involvement in Don's care. I couldn't stand aside and let anybody else make decisions—at least not without consulting me and making sure I understood that it was the best thing to do.

The abruptness and seemingly uncaring attitude of the few pushed me to where I needed to be so I could do a better job of helping care for Don. In retrospect, although I didn't like what happened, and they did upset me, in some ways they were a blessing.

We tend to think of blessings being the good things that come unexpectedly into our lives, and that's certainly one form. But there are other ways to be blessed, and sometimes we have to endure hardships before we realize that those trying events and people are meant to be God's pathway to blessing.

A verse from Hebrews reminded me that "no discipline is enjoyable while it is happening—it's painful! But afterward there will be a peaceful harvest of right living for those who are trained in this way" (12:11). *Discipline* isn't the word I would have used, and yet, in retrospect, that's probably an accurate description of my challenges. Those were the methods—the discipline—God used to change me and to force me to grow.

I say it this way: God uses the not-so-good things to rub off rough edges and to make us more sensitive or cause us to become aware of bigger issues. Some of the lessons even make us more responsible in the tasks we have.

21.

THE SILENT TREATMENT

We didn't have to pay any of the hospital bills. It was such a relief to me to learn that everything was fully covered. It took so much pressure off me; I could hardly believe it. Our lawyer told me that between our insurance and the State of Texas, all costs would be covered. "You should also get some kind of settlement from the State."

I didn't understand how that worked, so my lawyer asked me to come to his office so that he could explain. Texas law requires permission from the State before someone can sue. Furthermore, the State of Texas has a limit on the amount of compensation they will pay.

"What they offer won't even cover the hospital bills," he said. Before I could ask questions, he continued, "That's where workers' compensation fits in. They will cover whatever is unpaid. Your husband was working—he was on the way from a church conference to his church—when the accident occurred."

I stared at him for a moment, and tears flowed. I felt such a sense of release from the tension and concern about money. I knew there would be bills of hundreds of thousands—perhaps half a million dollars in medical bills. Now I understood that when God had said,

"Everything is going to be all right," it wasn't just about Don's survival. He meant *everything*, including the hospital bills.

———

On Tuesday, after Don's Sunday move to St. Luke's, I was back in my classroom. It seemed important to me to establish a routine. Once I did that, I was able to adjust to the way things happened in our lives.

Five mornings a week I got out of bed, ate breakfast, cleaned up, dressed, went to school, and arrived no later than seven thirty. I taught until two o'clock because I was free for the last hour, and the principal didn't insist on my staying until the children left. I immediately drove up Highway 288 toward the medical center. Typically it took me about thirty minutes to reach the hospital parking deck. I tried to get to the room before three. I stayed at the hospital until eleven o'clock each evening, when they forced all visitors to leave.

I wanted my life to become routine and predictable, and in many ways it was. But trying to get papers graded and doing the paperwork all teachers have to do was hectic. Some days I felt overwhelmed. I didn't say much, but the other teachers must have sensed the tension of my situation.

"Don't worry about that," a team member would say. "We've got it covered."

"I can correct those papers for you," another one might offer.

I'm grateful for them because they carried a large part of the load for me. I hated writing lesson plans, but that's one of the ongoing tasks for teachers. As much as possible, my fellow teachers took over the mundane activities or the nonteaching responsibilities.

Each morning, once the children arrived at Stevenson Primary School, everything changed for me. I was able to push away my anxiety (most of the time) or at least stop constantly thinking of Don. I tried to stay focused on my students.

By Texas law, teachers have a duty-free lunch. That means for thirty minutes each day our kids went to the cafeteria, and we didn't have to be with them. The schools hire aides to watch them during the lunch period.

Most of the time we ate in the teacher's lounge and were able to spend the time with other adults. It was a good change for me to be away for half an hour. It was the middle of the day, and the other teachers behaved as if they sincerely wanted to be kept abreast of developments.

Stevenson Primary is a public school, but most of the teachers were Christians and active in church. Several of the teachers went to our church, as did our principal. In that informal setting it was no problem to talk about God at work in our lives.

I didn't mind their questions because they showed me they were concerned and eager to do anything they could to help me. They reached out, and I was a sister, so they took care of me. Just as important, they always seemed eager to hear about any progress, no matter how minor it might be.

Every day when I went in for lunch, I received the same questions, and I believe they were heartfelt, although it sometimes wore me out to go through the same ritual day after day.

"How is Don doing?"

"What's the latest update?"

They also had a few questions or comments about how I was holding up—and that helped.

"How are you doing, Eva?" "Are you able to handle all this stress?" "Are you getting enough sleep?"

I would give them simple, innocuous answers.

Sometimes another teacher would ask, "How do you do it?"

"With God," I often said, and meant it. "I'm not doing this by myself. I'm doing this with God's help."

Regularly I had reminders from fellow teachers of their concern. "I'm praying for you and Don every day." "We pray for you every Sunday in church." One Roman Catholic teacher, knowing my Baptist background, said, "I hope you don't mind: I lit a candle for Don at mass."

I was humbled by her statement and thanked her profusely.

After my half-hour break, it was back to the classroom, and I usually felt refreshed. I taught until two. Within minutes of that I would be inside my car and on the highway to the medical center.

After I arrived at Don's floor, I stopped at the nurses' station to ask how Don had done that day. Over the days and weeks Don was a patient, I made an effort to know the staff. I began by thanking them when they came to the room. I wanted them to know I appreciated everything they were doing to help Don. It didn't matter if it was an RN or a custodian; everyone had a role in making life easier. Because I took the time to appreciate their efforts, we developed good relationships. I tried never to be demanding or condescending.

Don benefited from my efforts, and so did I. While I occasionally heard the nurses complain about certain patients or roll their eyes when the call bell lit up, if we needed anything, it was done as quickly as possible. Don often received extra care because of the rapport I had established. The staff always made sure I had enough pillows and blankets if I was spending the night. Because I took the time to care about them, Don and I were treated as part of the floor family.

On my daily visits to the hospital, once I got information from the nurse, I walked into the room and said hello to Don. Most of the time there was no response. He lay flat, staring at the ceiling, or his eyes would be closed. When I tried to engage him in conversation, he rarely acknowledged my words. Most of the time he turned his head away from me.

I made a point of repeating to Don what I heard from the duty nurse and always hoped it would cheer him up a little.

It didn't.

I usually asked, "Did you eat today?" If he answered, I tried to get him to tell me more, such as whether he had an appetite. "Did you have therapy today? Did Dr. Greider come by? Did you have a bowel movement?"

That last one may seem like a strange question, but because of

Don's prolonged horizontal position, his inability to move, and large doses of medication, many of his bodily systems weren't functioning properly. Each new problem required different approaches to ease them. Everything seemed important. Or perhaps I just wanted him to show he appreciated my being there and expressing my concern.

His system had shut down. He was in a heavy depression, and I didn't know what that was or how to help him. I cried often but didn't raise my voice.

Don had three basic responses. He might growl, and it sounded like a form of yes. Or he turned his face away. The third response was to lie unmoving, as if I had said nothing, or he hadn't heard me.

If he had treated everyone the way he did me, it probably wouldn't have been so painful. He didn't treat the nursing staff with the same coldness. When they came into his room and asked him questions, he responded. He used whole sentences. There wasn't much expression in his voice, but there was communication.

As soon as the staff person left, he was back to staring at the ceiling. The TV was always on, and he often turned his face to stare at the set.

He wouldn't talk to me.

I realize now that Don's behavior wasn't anger against me. His depression was so overpowering that he could be himself only with me. That may sound strange, and I didn't figure it out for a long time. He was a minister, a public person, and he had been trained to respond to others. With me Don could be himself. In my presence he didn't have to hide his depression.

Even if I had understood, I would still have been hurt.

During the first days I didn't say much when Don didn't answer. I wanted to ask, "Why don't you talk to me?" But I didn't know if that would help or impede his recovery, so I kept quiet.

For a while.

I couldn't figure out then what was going on inside Don. He certainly didn't have to perform for me. I don't think he was aware how he behaved toward me and didn't realize that his silence cut me out of his life.

I left at the end of visiting hours and usually cried most of the way home as I drove along the darkened highway. I felt utterly alone and hurt. Sometimes I banged on the steering wheel and screamed at the top of my voice. I hated the way I felt—the anger, the frustration, and the feeling that Don didn't love me anymore.

Although I didn't voice my feelings to him, inwardly I asked, *Why don't you talk to me?* After a number of silent-treatment days, I became frustrated and angry. Finally, I said, "You don't seem to appreciate that you're alive. You shut me out and won't talk to me. I'm here. I love you and I care, but you don't do anything except give me the silent treatment."

He turned his head away from me.

As the one who watched him, I was grateful that God had spared his life. Shouldn't he be grateful? Why didn't he seem happy to be alive? He was in pain, but he was breathing. Wasn't that worth something? *What's wrong with him? He acts as if he resents being alive. How could he not be grateful?*

He had been in a horrific accident and declared dead by emergency technicians, and yet he survived. He was back with his wife and his children. By now the doctors felt reasonably sure they could save his leg.

He was going to be all right—not as healthy as he had been before—but functional and able to go back to his work as a youth pastor. I reminded myself of those words God had whispered to me at school right after the accident. I couldn't understand why he was so low and unresponsive.

As the days passed, Don got even worse.

I didn't know at the time about the miracle after the accident. Had I known earlier that he'd actually gone to heaven, I might have felt differently. But because I didn't know, I felt resentful, especially when he talked to strangers or the nurses but not to his own wife.

I couldn't understand, and that troubled me and upset me. Finally I became angry enough to tell him. I never yelled, but I spoke to him, sometimes in strong, firm words—what I might call my teacher's voice.

"You've got to do this." "Why aren't you answering me?" "Don't you care what happens to you? To me and to the children?"

He didn't respond to any of my pleadings.

When visitors came or I spoke to anyone on the phone, the first question was nearly always, "How is Don doing?"

I decided not to cover up for him. When they asked, I said, "He doesn't seem to care."

And yet when visitors came to the room and asked Don how he was doing, he answered in short, positive statements.

"All right."

"I'm getting better."

"It's a slow process."

Although I was delighted that he responded to them, it made me feel even worse that he blocked me out. He was polite to others, although he wasn't very open and said little. With his intense pain that was understandable. *But he talked.*

To others.

If he could do that for them—people far less important to him, why wouldn't he talk *to me*? He was downright mean to me by his absolute lack of response.

A natural reaction was to wonder what I had done wrong. I searched my heart and could think of nothing. We certainly hadn't argued before the accident.

Dad was my best source of encouragement, and his weekly presence calmed me. I could also open up to him. He and Mom took a huge load off me. Each Friday afternoon, Dad and Mom would pick up the twins and drive for about six hours to reach our house. In 1989, that was a long trip because they had to travel on two-lane roads, which are now four-lane.

Joe hates to be inside a car—he's always been that way. So he had a difficult time riding all those hours. Mom and Dad made extra stops to let Joe escape the confines of the car.

I'm grateful to my parents for showing up every weekend. They slept at our house. The Mauldins brought Nicole to the house Friday night so she could stay with her brothers for the weekend.

Saturday morning Mom and Dad brought Nicole and the twins to the hospital. *Surely Don will talk to them*, I thought.

I was shocked, but Don treated the children the same way he did me. He acted as if he didn't care whether they came. He probably never said more than ten words to the children.

They stayed an hour, or perhaps two at most, and the twins were ready to go back to Shreveport. I'm not sure how aware they were of their father's lack of response. I assumed they thought he was in pain and didn't feel like talking.

When it was obvious that Joe and Chris were ready to leave, Dad would say, "Okay, kids, it's time to get back on the road. We don't want to tire out your father."

My dad observed how Don treated me, even though I didn't say much about it. It upset him because, like me, he felt Don ought to be grateful and excited to be alive and couldn't understand his terrible, downcast attitude.

One time, Dad leaned over to Don and asked quietly, "Why are you acting like this?"

"I don't deserve this," Don said slowly. "I don't deserve to be in this pain."

"That's right. You deserve to be dead!"

Don turned his face away.

Don did deserve to be dead, of course. There was no medical reason he should have survived the accident.

My dad wasn't trying to be mean; he was in his protective-father mode. He saw how hurt I was. I think he was trying to shock Don into being grateful for being alive.

Often while my parents stayed in the room with Don, the kids and I went downstairs to the McDonald's on the first floor. I thought it strange that St. Luke's had a McDonald's, but I learned to appreciate it being there.

In McDonald's I could visit with my kids and catch up on their lives. It was the one place we could be together and leave the sights and smells of the hospital behind. Their presence lifted my spirit and gave me a real feeling of inner peace and sometimes joy. It was great to hear the boys fuss about having to do homework or express their excitement because Grandpa had taken them to the lake. Nicole might share about the new music her choir was working on or the boy she currently liked.

I stared at their faces and tried to soak up every feature. I knew they would be leaving soon and I wouldn't see them for another week. But while we sat in McDonald's, we were a regular family at a fast-food restaurant. Before the accident I would never have dreamed how much I could enjoy a cheeseburger and fries.

———

I was becoming worn-out by the rigid, day-after-day (and night-after-night) schedule. I stayed in Don's room until eleven o'clock. Sitting in that room alone with no words from Don made it even more difficult. I had school work, which helped, and I took time to eat in the cafeteria, but other than those twenty minutes, I was in that room every evening for nearly six hours. Writing in the journal was good therapy for me, but even that wasn't enough.

Nurses came in and went out. In the early days we had many evening visitors, but as I expected, the longer Don remained in the hospital, the less frequently friends came to see him.

Perhaps this sounds like grumbling, which is certainly not my intention. When visitors came, they spent most of their time focusing on Don. I appreciated their concern for him.

"Is there anything I can get you?" a few of them would ask me. "Anything you want me to bring you?" The most frequent question to me was, "Do you need anything?"

I admit that I became weary of responding to the do-you-need-anything question. It was the natural, obvious question, and our friends truly wanted to know. The fact that they asked showed their concern. Still, responding to the same question several times a day for weeks wasn't easy. So when they asked if Don or I needed anything, my usual answer was, "No, we're fine. Pray for us and we'll be good."

Two things I want to make clear. First, I was more worried about what needed to be done for Don than what needed to be done for me.

Second, I didn't want to impose on anyone. I find that's typical of most women. We try to be superwife, supermom, superemployee, and always alert and ready to handle whatever life throws at us.

I was wrong to react as I did, but I didn't know how to respond differently. I had to learn to allow caring friends to minister to me.

About the fourth or fifth week of Don's recovery, I received a warm scolding from Ginny Foster—and I deserved it. "You need to let people help you."

"But I don't want to—"

Ginny stared right into my face. "You have to let some people help you because you need time to recharge your batteries."

"I know, but—"

"You can't take care of Don if you don't take care of yourself." Then she said something startling. "If you don't let them do something for you, you're robbing them—"

"Robbing them?"

"You're stealing the opportunity for them to help. If you let them do something—anything—you're not only making them feel appreciated; you're giving them the opportunity to serve."

She was right, but I still resisted.

I had to force myself to open up to them—and had to be exhorted several times before the message penetrated. Ginny's exhortation probably did the most for me because I hadn't thought of *their* needs. Perhaps that sounds odd, but when I looked at it as my way to help them, I could allow them to do something for me.

I don't think I'm much different from most people, and they tend to react as I did. So now, when I encounter others who have to walk in the dark as I did, I urge them, "Let people help. It may not be easy or comfortable, and you probably want to resist asking for help. Don't."

My cowriter said, "The most loving thing I can do for others is to let them express their love to me." That sounds simple, and it is—if we're open to hear.

Ginny had been right to scold me. She'd also said, "It won't feel natural to you, but you have to start somewhere. Say yes to anything, no matter how small or simple the gesture." A short time after that conversation, I decided to give others permission to help and put it into action. An elderly couple came to visit. They talked to Don and to me. We had a nice, quiet time together, and they didn't stay long. It was obvious they were ready to leave, so they asked Don, "Do you need anything?"

He shook his head and said, "No, nothing."

The husband turned to me. "Is there anything we can get you?"

Rather than decline, I said, "You know what? I would love a Diet Coke from McDonald's."

"I'll bring it up right away," he said. "Anything else you'd like with that?"

"A Diet Coke is enough."

Within minutes he handed me the cup. That was the best Diet Coke I've ever tasted. Or at least the most I've ever appreciated it. And from the joyful expression on his face when he handed the drink to me, it seemed as if he had presented me with the nectar of the gods. I knew I had done something to help him too. For people like me, serving others seems so much more important than taking care of myself by letting others help. By reframing the idea, I realized the importance of what that elderly man did.

That was one more lesson I had to learn as I struggled through the darkness.

After that, I contrived needs or excuses whenever anyone asked. "I'd like a magazine, if you don't mind. I haven't done any pleasure reading for days."

Not only did I enjoy what others did for me, but it made them feel good. It was a joy to me to watch the delighted expressions on their faces when I told them things they could do. Both of us came out winners.

In some ways it does seem strange to talk about what I learned while I sat in the hospital room through all those evenings. I had things to learn even in the dark.

I was open to hear God speak. I didn't know where else to turn.

———

There was a second part to this lesson: I needed time to recharge my batteries. I had to learn to take time for myself.

Staying day and night at the hospital is draining on all levels. After a while it becomes harder and harder to concentrate and think, which disrupts your ability to make decisions. The away time doesn't have to be long; sometimes a simple walk down the hall is all that is required.

I found my recharge in various ways. Sometimes as I was driving home, I found a radio station playing some of my favorite music, so I rolled down the window and sang at the top of my voice. While I was singing I wasn't thinking of the problems at the hospital.

Other times I found a quiet area and either prayed or read my Bible. Sometimes I simply sat and soaked up the quiet. I came to understand that my recharge times meant I would be in better shape to care for Don. My mind was clear, and I was refreshed.

———

The kindness of others didn't stop with that Diet Coke. They showed up at our house to vacuum or to dust. Men came to the house with their lawn mowers and cared for the yard. A group of friends purchased a parking pass for me so I didn't have to continue paying the fees at the parking garage.

Every once in a while someone would bring me a bag filled with snacks so I didn't have to keep going down to the vending machine. That was Ginny's specialty, but a few others did it as well.

As I've pointed out elsewhere, teachers at Stevenson Primary School did so much for me. I taught each day, but several of them graded the papers. They wrote lesson plans. Even more significant, they did something that was memorable for me and for our family.

When they first heard of Don's accident, my fellow teachers went to the dollar store and bought a variety of kid treasures—those little junk kinds of things that kids love: stickers, small rubber balls, card games, crayons, coloring books, hair ribbons, cheap fingernail polish, small plastic toys, mini puzzles, and books. They wrapped each item and labeled it either "Nicole," "Chris," or "Joe," and filled up a large box. They left the box at our house.

My mom was there that day, and every morning thereafter the kids had a little present when they got up for breakfast. Those simple gifts helped our kids know they were being thought of, and it gave them a joyful way to start their day.

The kids loved their little daily treats, and those teachers' gestures brought great peace to me. When they did those things for the children, they were doing wonderful things for Don and for me. Whenever I tended to get down or feel sorry for myself, I thought of the faculty at school or people at church who did so many little things to help us through that dark period.

22.

NICOLE IS GROWING UP

In February 1989, only weeks after Don's accident, Nicole was in her second semester of junior high school. February means a Valentine's Day dance. This would be her first dance, and a young man from her school had invited her to go with him. We were fine with that, and they, along with some of their friends, planned to attend as a group.

Don had barely gotten out of intensive care by Valentine's Day, and I remained at the hospital every night. Nicole needed attention to help her make it a special occasion. I didn't know what to do. I wanted the dance to be special for her, but I didn't know how. How could I leave Don? Yet there was so much I wanted to do to help make it a big event for our daughter.

Nicole is our only daughter, and I remembered how special my first dress-up event had been for me. I wanted her to have those same special memories.

I was torn between the responsibilities of being a wife and those of being a mother. To her credit, Nicole never pushed me or complained. But I often beat myself up knowing I wasn't there for my children. Kids grow up fast, and I didn't want to miss being part of the important events in their lives. It hurt to think she might miss out on creating a beautiful memory.

To my delight, one of the church secretaries took it upon herself to pick up Nicole from school, drive her to the mall, and buy her a new dress and shoes with matching jewelry. She also made sure that on the day of the dance, Nicole had her hair done.

Our daughter said she felt like a princess. Afterward, looking at pictures from the dance confirmed those feelings.

Not only was I delighted for Nicole and grateful to the secretary, but it was special for me because I was able to stay at the hospital.

Today if anyone asks Nicole about major events in her life at that time, that's probably right there in the list of her top memories—or at least I know it is in mine. That sensitive, caring secretary must have sensed how important it was to our daughter. She made Nicole's first dance very, very special. She made a mother grateful.

I point out these things because they're what I call the life-support system that we needed and that sustained us through the worst part of Don's recovery. So many people reached out to us and took a tremendous amount of pressure off me.

When I speak to people about my own walk in the dark, I try to make an important point: "You have to be a friend to have a friend." Don and I had tried to be open to others and share what we could of ourselves. We didn't do it to receive anything in return. And yet, when we were in need, people remembered and responded. "You need to start building those relationships today," I say. "Don't wait until you have a life crisis to put your life-support system in place."

Like that secretary. Like Ginny and Susan and Suzan.

Several times tears filled the eyes of a friend who brought something for us. With variations, here's something I heard many times as my friends handed me a gift or brought me a book to read: "It isn't much, but you gave me an opportunity to tell you how important you've been in my life."

They didn't repay us—they overpaid us with kindness and love. I also point out in my talks that such wonderful blessings don't happen from nowhere; they come out of the context of living.

I've often thought of Jesus' words, "Give, and you will receive. Your gift will return to you in full—pressed down, shaken together to make room for more, running over, and poured into your lap" (Luke 6:38). That's how it works for Christians. We give because we see a need and it's the right thing to do. God keeps score and raises up those who can help us when we're the needy ones.

In some ways we gave others permission to help us by setting the example. It's like building a safety net. Jesus gave us the golden rule: "Do to others whatever you would like them to do for you" (Matt. 7:12).

It's not only a divine principle but it's also a practical one. The more freely we give, the more generously others give to us. I like to think that God keeps score and is more generous in his giving than we are in ours.

We never know when tragedy will strike when we give of ourselves. When those terrible times come, we're "insured" because we've paid our premiums forward.

I sometimes worry that the use of various social networks causes many to lose their personal connections with others. Nothing can take the place of a face-to-face conversation or at least hearing a loved one's voice on the phone. Further, to make others respond to us without begging for help, we have to be involved in their lives and sensitive to their needs—whether it's a family member, a friend, or a neighbor. Our family had made the effort to spend time with our friends and family; we invested time with them. For people who already knew me, helping out was their way of ministering to me or returning my "investment" in them.

It wasn't only friends. Our family jumped in. As I've mentioned, my parents took the boys. Don's mother stayed with him in the summer of 1989 so I could take Don's place and drive kids to youth camp.

Others—total strangers to us—ministered to us in many ways. They saw places where they could help, and they did.

I received so many kind gifts of time and material blessings, but even more, people gave of themselves, which was even better. Until the accident, I didn't realize how important it was to receive.

I was grateful each time, but I didn't reflect on those things during the first months after Don's accident. I was consumed with making it through each day and holding our family together.

Once I was able to pause and reflect, however, I couldn't possibly overestimate the value of other people. Many times I've said and truly meant it, "I don't know how we could have survived that first year without other people."

I also realize that my upbringing helped me appreciate the importance of others. My father was in the air force for more than twenty years. That meant we moved fairly frequently. Because of those moves I was aware how important it was to make friends and connections, so I learned to reach out to others. If I had waited for everyone to come to me, I would have remained a very lonely girl.

Being part of a military family also meant that most of my friends were of different backgrounds. Through the military we shared common interests and lifestyles. We strengthened and encouraged each other. We developed friendships quickly and deeply and treasured them while we were together.

I'm sure that's why we connected with so many and the reason I saw the importance of others who reached out to me. To have a friend, I had to be a friend.

The best way for me to say this in the way of advice is this: *Be there*. Be aware. Watch for those often small opportunities to show compassion and to express concern. What may seem little to us when we do it may be an immense blessing to the recipients.

I realized this when I thanked people for their help. "It was such a small thing," was a common response. "I didn't do much," was another. From their perspective that was probably true. But in our eyes—the receivers'—they gave so much, and at times their generosity overwhelmed us.

I don't want this to sound depressing—as if life is constantly trying to knock us down. That's not my intention. But life does have a way of turning upside down for each of us at some point or at many points. That's when we need help—not only from God but from the people he uses.

———

Those first days with Don in the ICU obviously made the strongest impression. One of the terms I heard daily was *life support*. And in the ICU, that's critical.

I've thought a great deal about those two words. And I've used the term for more than the ICU or the critical care unit. All of us need life support. At some point in our lives we need that "something extra" we can't provide for ourselves.

My cowriter says it this way: "If you live long enough, you will take care of someone, or someone will take care of you." Don and I experienced that at a relatively young age. I hope I never forget the lessons.

In the hospital, life support means the body can't support itself and needs extra help to boost it so it can function. We don't like depending on machines or on other people, but sometimes it's the only way we can make it through our dark times. My strong family connections as well as our friends from church, my school, and our neighborhood provided that life support for me. I'll always be grateful.

23.

A STRANGE COMFORT

Toward the end of February, I once again made the forty-five-minute drive from Alvin to St. Luke's Hospital. I parked the car, crossed the street, entered the hospital, and walked down the long hallway to the yellow elevators. When the doors opened, I hit the button for the twenty-first floor. That was my daily routine. I had come from school, and I spent the entire evening with Don saying nothing to me.

As awful as it may sound, it was like talking to a zombie. I felt there was no humanity—no emotion—left in him. He was a body lying there with a heavy metal cage around his left side. He showed no warmth or even the slightest emotion.

One event was so powerful I have to tell about it. The school day had been difficult. The weight of constant driving, little sleep, and teaching each day was taking its toll. I was exhausted on all levels. That evening, for the first time, I decided to go home early from the hospital.

I picked up my school bag, headed toward the door, and then turned to tell my husband good night and that I would see him the next day. As usual I received no response.

Something snapped in me. I had reached the end of my patience. I can see myself clearly. I was wearing a pink jumper with a cream-colored shirt underneath and had my school bag on my arm.

I walked to the foot of his bed and stared right at him. "I'm tired of this. You don't seem to care about anything. You don't care that you're back with us. You don't care about the kids when they come to see you. You're being mean!"

I turned away and that's when I saw his reflection in the mirror. Tears were streaming down his face. Don was crying.

I felt terrible. I put down my school bag, walked around, and as best I could, I put my arms around him. "It's going to be okay. We'll make it through this." I was comforting him as I would a hurting child.

In the early years of our marriage, Don often put his arms around me as I silently sobbed over some problem at work or an insecurity I felt. In his arms I found a sense of protection and comfort. Now the roles were reversed. Even though his body was wrapped in hideous metal, as best I could, I wrapped my arms around him while the tears flowed down his cheeks, his chest heaving as he cried silently. My tears mixed with his.

Don said nothing more, but something happened to me. *For the first time* I realized how difficult it was for him. I knew he was in pain, but I hadn't grasped the effects of the pain.

I sat back down on the sofa next to his bed. He didn't say another word to me, and I didn't say anything to him. Perhaps I was ashamed.

His tears had changed everything. And I was comforted.

24.

DON'S STORY

As many people already know, Don had a remarkable experience in the accident. He died.

It's important to make this point. It was not what we call a near-death experience (NDE) or some kind of coma. All the medical evidence supports this fact.

My cowriter, Cecil Murphey, who also helped Don write *90 Minutes in Heaven*, at first doubted the story and wasn't interested in writing the book. "I'm not interested in a near-death story," he told Don.

"I *died*. I didn't pass through a dark tunnel or see light," Don insisted. "I didn't float above the people and the wreckage. I had none of those experiences associated with NDE."

Cec still wasn't convinced. "Let me pray about it, and let's talk later." Don and Cec e-mailed and phoned each other several times, beginning in 2003.

"He finally convinced me by giving me two facts," Cec said. The EMTs were professionals, and if there had been any pulse, even a small one, surely they would have detected it. If Don had been alive during those ninety-plus minutes, his heart would have been pumping blood, and he would have bled to death from his massive, gaping wounds.

"Second, I know that we can deprive our brains of oxygen about four minutes, but when we reach six minutes, we're in a vegetative state. After that, there's no resuscitation. Yet there was no brain damage. That makes it a believable miracle for me."

Don went immediately to the gates of heaven and stayed there until another minister, Dick Onarecker, came along and prayed him back to earth.**

Later, Cec was able to point out the similarity of Don's experience with that of the apostle Paul. "Don has never claimed to have superior visions or greater understanding than others, but his account squares with Paul's."

Here's the biblical record:

> I will reluctantly tell about visions and revelations from the Lord. I was caught up to the third heaven fourteen years ago. Whether I was in my body or out of my body, I don't know—only God knows. . . . I do know that I was caught up to paradise and heard things so astounding that they cannot be expressed in words, things no human is allowed to tell. . . . I don't want anyone to give me credit beyond what they can see in my life or hear in my message, even though I have received such wonderful revelations from God. So to keep me from becoming proud, I was given a thorn in my flesh, a messenger from Satan to torment me and keep me from becoming proud. (2 Cor. 12:1–7)

Although we don't know what Paul meant by a "thorn in my flesh," many scholars believe it was a physical impediment, probably an eye disease.

After Don had been on the road, sharing his experience with others, he once told Cec, "I've met about thirty other people who've had experiences similar to mine."

** You can read the entire account in *90 Minutes in Heaven* by Don Piper with Cecil Murphey (Grand Rapids, MI: Revell), 2004.

I wanted to make that background clear so others can understand Don's postsurgical depression. I didn't understand what was going on. On some level I sensed something had happened to him during the accident, but I had no idea what it was. As he would tell me and others later, he'd gone into full-scale, clinical depression. "I didn't want to live," he said, "and I was angry to be alive." For weeks he wasn't aware of the depression because the physical ordeal prevented him from thinking about the cause.

Social workers, who were actually therapists, came to help Don work through his depression. Even though they didn't tell us they were therapists, Don saw right through them and their approach. He gave them the answers he knew they wanted. I don't think they did him much good, and they eventually stopped visiting.

Don was angry—a lot. He wasn't angry with God, although he often wondered why God would send him back to earth and force him to go through such intense physical suffering. He took out his anger on me and the rest of the family.

It took a while, but I finally came to understand that Don acted that way toward us because he didn't feel he had to put on a show of normalcy for us. With us he could act the way he really felt because he knew we loved him. Even that knowledge didn't soothe the hurt Don sometimes caused. I'm sure my husband never felt he was taking his frustration out on us, but that feeling was very real to me.

I loved him but I didn't like him very much during those times. It occurred to me that God loves us in all our ugliness. I decided to try to see Don through God's eyes. I could forgive him because I loved him even when his words hurt.

At times he reacted unenthusiastically to the staff, even though he knew they were doing their best. Don wasn't ever suicidal, but he was severely depressed, not knowing when or if he would ever lead a normal life again. The recuperating wasn't worth the pain. At times he prayed to die and begged God to take him.

One early morning before dawn, he couldn't sleep and was

listening to CDs. The Imperials singing "Praise the Lord" caught his attention. After that he heard the David Meece song that says, "We are the reason that He gave His life." ***

As Don thought about those words, he did something that's rare for him: he cried.

Tears slid down his cheeks for a long, long time. Calmness followed, and the depression lifted.

———

I didn't know about Don's heavenly journey and his terrible disappointment with having to be back on earth. Had I known, perhaps I could have been more sympathetic.

"Were you worried about what was going to happen?" a number of people have asked.

"I don't know," I've often replied, and that was an honest answer. I've learned that when I'm in a crisis situation, I don't have time to think about what's going to happen in the future. Whether that's a gift or a curse, I focus on what's happening right there, at that minute.

At times we encountered those minute-to-minute situations. On only a few, rare occasions, I recall thinking about what would happen next. Instead of wondering, *What's going to happen next?* my question was, *What needs to happen* now? *What do I need to do* now *to help Don get better?*

What energy I had, I spent taking care of the crisis at that moment. Matthew 6:34 says, "Don't worry about tomorrow, for tomorrow will bring its own worries." That's good counsel.

During the first two or three surgeries, it was comforting to have close friends sit with me in the surgical waiting area. I especially appreciated Cliff sitting with me on the night Don was brought to the

---

*** "We Are the Reason," words and music by David Meece, copyright 1980, Meece Music (admin. by Word Music).

hospital. As the number of surgeries wore on, I became a proficient waiting-room professional. I knew which chairs were the most comfortable, which area was the quietest, and where the restrooms and vending machines were located.

I was even on a first-name basis with the volunteers who came through with carts full of muffins and other pastries. It may sound strange, but sometimes I looked forward to spending time there. I knew Don was in good hands in the surgical suite, getting everyone's complete attention. I was close by if needed.

In Don's room I tried to grade papers or do other types of work, but always with a watchful eye to see if he needed anything. I could never really focus on what I was doing or have some uninterrupted quiet time. But in the waiting room, I had the chance to release Don into the capable hands of his doctor.

Many times people would tell me, "I'll be by to sit with you." It took a while for me to speak up, but I was finally able to say, "I appreciate that so much, but I'm fine. I'll call as soon as I know something." At first people protested, but finally most understood I was being straightforward.

That sounds simple, but it took a vast amount of energy and effort for me to take such a position. I didn't want to hurt people's feelings, but I didn't need or want a lot of people to sit with me.

I appreciated the time and effort it took for every person to drive to the hospital to check on us. What many visitors don't realize is how difficult it may be for the person who is waiting. Some individuals need others around them, and they thrive on the conversation because it keeps their minds focused. I didn't always need that. For me, it meant I had to entertain them. That may sound more negative than I intend. By entertaining, I mean that I had to stay engaged in conversation. Many visitors couldn't handle silence, and in their discomfort they kept words moving and often jumped from topic to topic. Perhaps they were nervous or anxious.

Sometimes I wanted a few minutes to relax and not concentrate on other people. Most of my evenings at the hospital, I had my school work with me and needed to grade papers and plan classwork. I wanted to do my Bible study and journaling. As soon as someone knocked on the door, I felt like a hostess who has guests in her house. I had to make them comfortable. It wasn't until later when I was worn-out that I realized I had expended a lot of energy talking to our visitors.

Another consideration is the patient. I know Don was using what little energy he had to recover. That is true of most who are in the hospital. Their get-up-and-go has got-up-and-went. This isn't to complain but to urge people to become more sensitive. A simple question would have helped. "Would you prefer to be alone? I see you're busy on school work, so I won't stay. I just wanted you to know I care." I probably would have put away the school work anyway, but then it would have been my choice.

Even better would be to call before coming to ask, "Is now a good time to visit?" That way no one feels obligated to accept visitors after they've made the effort to drive to the hospital.

Another thing I realized was that visitors felt they had failed or been ineffective if they stayed only five to ten minutes. Most of them seemed to believe they had to chat with me for at least fifteen minutes (although I didn't watch the time) and then apologize for leaving so soon. At the time I enjoyed participating in the discussion, but later I paid the price when I was unable to get much sleep dealing with the typical hospital interruptions.

"Visiting the hospital room," I tell people nowadays, "isn't the same as being a guest in someone's home. The best guests make their presence known, express their concern, and leave quickly."

And yet, they cared. I reminded myself that they wouldn't have made the effort to visit if they hadn't cared.

25.

FROM INSIDE THE
HOSPITAL ROOM

During those days in the hospital (and even after Don came home), friends asked me, "How did you do it? How did you hold your job, take care of three children, and stay with Don?"

At the time it didn't seem to be any heroism on my part, and it doesn't now. I did what I needed to do. I had to work because the school position paid our insurance premiums. I had to care for my children, although my parents as well as our friends the Mauldins did so much to alleviate that burden.

I have a simple answer, and it's one I truly mean: *God.* I usually go on to say that God always sent me the right person at the right time who would say the right thing when I needed to hear it. A few times I'd sink low, and the Lord would send someone into the hospital room who would give me a hug or say a few kind words. I believe these folks were human angels of God, even though they had no awareness of being on a mission.

I wanted people to look directly at me and ask, "How are you?" That's when I sensed they meant their words. It certainly made the difference to me at the hospital. I heard the how-are-you-doing words often enough, but I didn't always hear the concern in the way the person asked them. When spoken right, that simple question can be sustaining—at least it was for me.

Often visitors quoted Scripture to me. I'm not against learning and quoting Bible verses. I have learned many, but I want to use them at exactly the right time. I wouldn't ever want God's words to come off as flippant or superficial.

Along with the words is the need for human touch: a hug if that's comfortable, a handshake, or even a light tap on the shoulder. There's something powerful about one human touching another, and it draws us to each other.

That reminds me of an old story about the little boy who was afraid of the dark. His father tried to explain to him there was nothing to fear. The boy was still afraid.

"Jesus is always with you," the father said.

"I know, Daddy," the boy replied, "but I want someone with skin on him."

Little boy or grown woman, we need the skin against skin when we're going through difficulties or trauma.

At times I felt as if my own darkness would never end. I often thought of the image of the roller coaster. Good news would send my spirits upward; then, only hours later, a report would come in that some other symptom had developed or that Don had an infection on his leg because someone hadn't taken proper care of the pins. Then I'd plummet to an emotional low.

One day I would arrive at the hospital feeling lighthearted and joyful, praising God that Don was improving. The next day, when I reached the nurses' station, I'd hear, "Your husband had a minor setback." It may have been minor for them, but even a minor setback is major for those who sit at the bedside. My spirits would drop, and often I'd pray silently, *How long, O Lord, will this go on?*

One of the worst setbacks came after Don was placed in the

Ilizarov frame. Every day a nurse came into his room and cleaned and disinfected the pinholes so his skin wouldn't attach itself to the wires (it happened a few times anyway). The nurse poured hydrogen peroxide down each hole, and that in itself exacerbated the pain. Then she'd clean the pinholes with Q-tips. Dr. Greider had explained the importance of using a new Q-tip for each pinhole to reduce the possibility of cross-contamination.

One time a nurse didn't clean the pinholes properly. She reused the Q-tips, and Don got an infection. Those pins went all the way through the femur and out the other side, where they were attached on the other side of the ring. Therefore, the infection could go to the bone, which is extremely dangerous. Two things could have resulted. First, in his weakened condition the infection could have spread rapidly, and he would have lost his leg despite everything he had already gone through. Or the more drastic result was that we could have lost Don.

The doctor moved Don to an isolation room to prevent the infection from spreading. We had to wear gowns and masks to go in his room. Visitors were limited, to reduce the risk of further contamination. I'm thankful the infection was cleared up in a few days, but that was a very frightening time.

———

Another serious mishap occurred in March. Don had improved enough that staff could get him up and put him in a wheelchair every day. That enabled his system to work better because God designed our bodies to work in a vertical position, not horizontal.

Because of the leg being encased in that halo device, they had to take a pillowcase and loop it through the fixator and then tie it to the leg extension part of the wheelchair so his leg wouldn't fall off the chair. That was necessary because he couldn't control his leg and certainly didn't have the strength to hold it in that position.

One time a nurse forgot to tie his leg to the wheelchair and the leg fell. The jolt of the leg dropping ripped the pinholes open. Not only was there terrible pain for Don, but blood spattered all over the area.

That was one of the worst days for him and certainly for me after I heard about it. That's what I mean by the roller-coaster effect. Don would improve nicely, and then there would be an accident or he wouldn't respond as his doctor hoped.

My initial reaction to the accident was to say to myself, "We've come this far and now what?" I swung into the downside of the loop and had to fight for inner peace.

Another frightening experience happened when Don began to develop bedsores. He was totally immobile, so the sores began to break out along his back. We again faced the risk of infection.

Because no one but Don had ever had the device on his femur, it took some time to come up with a plan. Doctors finally ordered a special mattress, designed with different chambers that alternated releasing and refilling with air. That way the pressure points were relieved along Don's back, and the sores began to heal, though he was still subjected to more irritation and pain.

Since the mattress created whooshing sounds as it went through its cycle, I had one more interruption to any sleep I was trying to get. For a time it seemed as if for every two steps we went forward, we fell three steps backward. The darkness would flicker between shades of black.

———

The Ilizarov apparatus, along with the arm fixator, were the most difficult parts of Don's recovery. Yet, as awful as they looked and as much pain as they gave him, they also brought peace to me. I knew there would eventually be an end to the treatment. One day a still-alive Don would leave the hospital, and I was sure he would walk again on his own two feet. I wouldn't have consented to the surgery if I had felt differently.

I became increasingly calm over the issue of the fixator. But I still had three children, and I couldn't wipe them out of my mind. Even though I knew they were being cared for and loved, I wasn't the one doing the caring, and an undeserved sense of failure hit me several times every day.

I also thought of the children in my classroom. Once Don was stabilized at the hospital, I had returned to teaching. My life was filled with forcing myself to get up in the morning, calling to check on Don, and hurrying to a full day of classes. I worked hard at school all day. At dismissal time I grabbed my papers and books and drove to the hospital. I stayed by Don's bedside until the end of visiting hours, and then I drove home. I didn't get all the sleep I needed, but I was with my husband, and I wouldn't have wanted it any other way. I was exhausted. The strain was becoming more and more evident on me.

———

As I've thought about my feelings during those first months of Don's recovery, I've realized I felt a lot of frustration and anger with him for perhaps as long as eight months after the accident.

We went through the initial period where our energies, prayers, and emotions focused on getting him to live. I had to make decision after decision. I'd say I was in a survival mode as much as Don was, although our battles were different. I rarely thought about what was going to happen in a month, or even the next day. For at least the first two weeks, I focused on what was going to happen within the next five minutes.

I felt pulled constantly in those early days. Don was my primary concern, of course, but as I've mentioned, I also thought about our three children. I'm a mother, and I couldn't stop worrying about them. I constantly felt pulled between staying at the hospital around the clock and being at home.

In the middle of that, of course, was my work. I loved teaching and didn't want to lose the job. And if I lost it, our insurance would also be gone. Still, I didn't focus nearly as much on teaching as I did on Don and the kids. I didn't neglect the schoolchildren, but they were lower on my priority list.

What do we have to do to make Don want to live?

What do we have to do to get him to breathe?

What do we have to do to get him to eat more?

Those questions filled my mind.

———

Toward the end of March, we learned we could take Don home. That was exciting, and I don't think any news lifted me more. But he got another infection, and that delayed us three days.

The roller-coaster effect again.

We also faced another challenge we hadn't anticipated. We were living in a rented house in the town of Friendswood. We were leasing because we hadn't decided where to buy. It was a lovely house, and we enjoyed it, but we had one problem: immediately inside the front door was a wall, causing anyone who entered to have to turn before going into the rest of the house. That wouldn't work for Don because there wasn't enough space to turn him in his wheelchair with his extended leg. There was no way to bend that leg with the fixator on it. Because of that, we couldn't get him into the house, so we needed to make other arrangements. The floor plan of the house also meant we couldn't get the hospital bed into the living room, much less the bedroom. Going in through the back door wouldn't work either.

I'm glad I realized all that before I tried to bring him home.

Once again, Ginny Foster came to my aid. She was a Realtor, and as soon as I explained the situation, she said, "I'm sure we can take care of it for you."

And she did. Immediately she started looking for places for us to rent. She scoured the area and took me along to look at a few of them.

On the third day Ginny found us a rental house that was closer to the church than where we lived, and it had an accessible entry. As soon as I saw it, I knew that house was exactly right for us.

It was an older house and it was big. Located on a cul-de-sac, it had a large, fenced backyard. There were four large bedrooms, formal living and dining areas, and a paneled den. Outside the den was a screened, covered patio. I thought Don would like to be able to sit out there and enjoy some fresh air.

The best thing was the entry. It had a straight, wide opening that led directly past the formal dining room and immediately to the den right behind it. The other hallway was too narrow to get him back to the master bedroom, but we could get him into the den. We set up a hospital bed there. Don slept in that hospital bed from the time he came home through February 1990.

I made a video of the rest of the house because Don would be unable to go through the rooms himself. With the video he could at least see what each room looked like. It was good to have him home.

I leased the house. The owners of our previous leased home in Friendswood were kind enough to let us out of that contract after hearing the circumstances. Once again, God was putting things together for our good.

It was quite a task to get everything moved from one house to the other and get it set up. To say my plate was full would be an understatement. But God was there for me once again. What would we have done without our friends, especially our church friends? We didn't have to hire a moving company because the congregation jumped right in. Our special friends, the Longs and the Mauldins, were at the forefront.

Our church and school families volunteered to help pack, load, and unload boxes into our new home. Some even stayed to help put items away. Still, it was another weight on my already overloaded shoulders.

Even once Don was home, infections developed, and we had several trips back to the hospital. Some of his hospital stays lasted two weeks. I usually drove him there, and ambulances brought him home.

It was a strange situation. Our three kids were staying elsewhere, and I was trying to teach school, spend as much time with Don as possible, find a house, and get us moved before they released him from the hospital. It was a stressful time during the entire ordeal because there was so much to do, and I had to take charge of everything.

Finding and leasing a house was something Don would have done with little effort. It was one more thing I had to learn as I stumbled along in the dark. And it would be far from the last time I'd feel inadequate to cope.

I discovered that finding a home was only the first step. A lease is a legal document. I had never signed one before. I'm thankful I had Ginny, who talked me through the process. I also had to deal with transferring utilities. I made a promise never to be in such an awkward position again.

Don had often encouraged me to be involved in the business details of our home, but I hadn't been interested. It took a crisis to get me to pay attention to those important matters. From that time I have been involved in all decision-making processes, from buying a car to buying a house.

I sighed deeply when I thought about everything and how things were working. We had leased a new house and were able to break the lease on the old house. We moved into our new place, and our furniture was in place. Friends brought in food, and we were ready to bring Don home and move him inside even though it would be a house he had never seen before.

———

We wanted to make Don's homecoming as eventful as possible. I knew it would tire him to go from the hospital to the house. But it would also invigorate him. We hung yellow balloons out in front of the house. We also hung a banner made by the youth from the church that read, "Welcome Home!"

My parents came to Alvin and brought the boys. I checked Nicole out of school. It was understood, though, that the boys would return to Bossier with my parents, and Nicole would go back with the Mauldins. I wanted time for Don to adjust to being home and begin the recuperation process. But this was a day we had all waited for, and we all wanted—no, we *needed*—to be there.

The trip from the hospital to home tired him out, which I had anticipated. He wasn't very responsive, but from the smile on his face, I know he was glad to be there. I'm sure he was delighted to be out of the hospital and away from the constant coming and going of the staff.

The ambulance backed into the driveway. The driver and attendant opened the back doors and lifted Don from the back on a gurney. I flashed back to that January day when he'd arrived at Hermann Hospital in much the same way. But this time I had a big smile and a happy heart. The attendants rolled the gurney up the sidewalk into the house. They lifted Don into the hospital bed, checked his vitals, wished all of us well, and left.

Don was home.

Before leaving the hospital, we were able to arrange it so a visiting nurse would come every day to check on him. The first nurse who came taught me how to work the screws and clean the pinholes on Don's fixator.

I took over and did that task every day. I never considered it tedious. I liked doing it because it made me feel useful and gave me peace to know I was able to do something specific to speed Don's recovery. It wasn't a task every person can do. I have a pretty strong stomach, and I could handle about anything.

Each time I had to press a Q-tip into a pinhole and turn the screws, pain spread across Don's face. He never cried out or complained, but he grimaced. I tried not to look at him but kept my gaze focused on the device instead. We assumed there wasn't anything more now than Don's slow progress toward getting well.

I wasn't out of the darkness yet.

———

It was easier for me with my husband at home. Not having to face the daily drive to St. Luke's was a huge relief. That alone gave me an extra hour and a half—longer if there was traffic (and in Houston there's always traffic).

I was no longer living by myself; there was another person at home. Just having him there made me sleep better at night. I left the door open so I could hear him if he needed me. With young children I had learned to sleep light in case they made a noise. I did the same thing with Don, and it was better than being in the house alone.

In the morning I tiptoed through the den to check on him before I left for school. By that time of the morning, he had fallen asleep and would be breathing deeply. It was the only time of day I saw his face relax. I treasured that look all day.

At the end of the school day, I rushed home to see how the day had gone. Volunteers came in to be with Don each day after I left. It was enjoyable to be able to go to my own home, sit on my couch, eat at my table, and still be where I could provide care if needed.

I was no longer tied to a small room with few choices. I could watch the TV shows I wanted, read, or just sit without a nurse coming in every few hours to check Don's vitals. There was also the belief that Don would recuperate faster at home. At least I wanted that to be true, and it made me feel better to believe it.

Don's coming home wasn't perfect, but it was a great relief. Being in his own home, even though it was a different one, also raised his spirits. We had visitors, especially the first few days. But by the end of the week, as it had been at the hospital, the visits were fewer and shorter.

On the sixth day after Don came home, he began running a fever, and his face was flushed. When I laid the back of my hand on his forehead, I realized how hot his skin felt. Immediately, I called Dr. Greider.

"We'll send an ambulance," he said. "We need to get him back to the hospital."

Within ten minutes the ambulance arrived, and two EMTs rushed inside with a gurney. Soon they had Don inside the ambulance, and it roared off toward St. Luke's. I followed in my car.

It was almost like going over everything again. He had developed a serious infection, and they didn't want it to spread. They put Don back in an isolation room until the infection was gone and his body temperature was normal. After two days he went to a room again, where he stayed for three days.

His second trip home occurred near the end of April. By then Don had made excellent progress and, with help, he could get in and out of his wheelchair fairly easily. I say *fairly* easily because nothing was easy then. But we had a routine, and I knew exactly what to do and how much he could do.

After that it was more or less a permanent thing for him to be home. I write *more or less*, because he had short trips back to the hospital, and we never knew when something would go wrong again.

I prayed, quietly pleading for God to let him have no further setbacks.

———

One morning the sound of a lawn mower awakened me. "What's going on?" I asked aloud as I ran to the window. I looked outside and saw that two boys from the Mealer family were mowing our grass. We hadn't asked them (or anyone) to mow the lawn. In fact, I hadn't even thought about anything outside the house. Church members decided they wanted to help us, so they showed up with their mowers and went to work.

That's only one spontaneous act of kindness, but there were many. I couldn't begin to list them all. People saw our needs and responded even without our having to ask. I didn't like depending on people, but I was grateful for the help. Church people as well as friends from the school and community helped in so many ways.

For example, the doorbell would ring, and by the time I opened the door, no one would be standing there, but someone would have left a cooked dinner for us. That happened several times. Another time when I went to the door, two women from the church held large pots of food—enough both for that night and for a second meal from the leftovers.

Other times I'd open the door and the visitors would say, "We're here to take the boys swimming." Or a girl would leave her parents in the car, run up to the door, and say, "Is Nicole here? We want to take her shopping with us."

These types of events happened often enough to keep our spirits encouraged and let us know that people cared. Those kind, sensitive souls will never, never know how grateful we were for their help—especially because they did it without our asking.

That was a special lesson to me. I determined that whenever I had the chance, I would respond the same way. I would see a need and do what I could without asking or making the recipient feel uncomfortable.

And then, of course, there was the Don Patrol.

26.
THE DON PATROL

We jokingly called it the Don Patrol—something Ginny Foster organized. Each morning, shortly after I left for school, volunteers from the church showed up. I was away from the house about seven hours, and someone needed to be there to help. Don was totally helpless, not even able to get out of bed on his own.

We never once had to ask anyone to come.

Our volunteer might be a man or a woman, but someone came every day that I taught school. Although the faces varied, their purpose was to serve Don that day.

The volunteer of the day always had a key to our front door, which I assumed the Don Patrol passed around among themselves. He or she entered the house noiselessly.

Because Don still suffered from so much pain, his sleeping habits varied. By the time the Don Patrol was in action, he was falling into an exhausted sleep about two o'clock each morning. He'd wake about ten. The volunteer usually arrived before nine while he was still asleep, and he or she sat quietly and waited for Don to wake up.

For the first three weeks at home, Don was rarely out of bed.

Even when he was, most days it was for as little as five minutes. The Don Patrol was ready to serve in any way they could. They brought in the newspaper, cooked breakfast, made lunch, and prepared snacks. Whatever Don needed, they were eager to provide. They answered the doorbell to let the visiting nurse and the physical therapist into the house, and they answered the phone to shield Don from having to take calls to buy insurance or participate in some contest. Later, they even transported Don to and from doctors' appointments and water therapy.

Don didn't have to talk to the Don Patrol or try to entertain them. They didn't come for conversation, but only to help. When they weren't actively doing something for him, they stayed out of his immediate sight.

By the time I returned home around three thirty, the volunteer of the day had gone. I assumed the volunteer left because he or she knew I didn't want to come home and have to visit. That sounds like a small thing, but Ginny had set it up well. The Don Patrol people were there to serve as unobtrusively as possible. Even that little part of it was well thought out.

During the summer the Don Patrol stopped because I was able to do everything. When school started again in August, they surged back into action and continued until about the middle of November. That's when Don received his brace.

———

Don hated being in a situation where he couldn't do anything for himself. He didn't like people waiting on him. It was quite a shift for Don—from being a highly independent man to having everything done for him.

At the same time, he was excited about being out of the hospital. And I was glad to have him home, although his "bedroom" was in the front of the house and I slept in the back bedroom. But he was there and we were together again as a family.

Just as marvelous, at the end of May—a time of year that also helped raise his spirits—our boys came back from my parents' home. Nicole had moved back in earlier that month. We were all different because circumstances had changed us, but we were together.

The school year ended, which was good for all of us. We had the summer to learn to accept a new lifestyle together. As a mother, having the whole family under one roof was the most important part of bringing me peace, and I think a significant factor in Don's recuperation. It was a major step forward for all of us.

———

Being the conscientious person he is, once Don was home from the hospital, he wanted to go back to church immediately. I'm not sure why it was so pressing. Perhaps it was to assure himself that he could still minister to people. But another reason was that he would have an opportunity to thank the members for their support. We insisted he wait for a few weeks, and he did. But once he did return to church, it was a special event none of us will forget.

Because we didn't have a vehicle that could accommodate him, someone drove the church van to our house. The deacons had taken out the seats, and several of them came along that day to lift Don, wheelchair and all, into the van. I put our three kids in our car and followed.

After we arrived at the church and Don and his wheelchair were lifted out of the van, I pushed him, and our kids fell in behind me. We walked to the side entrance, and a deacon opened the door.

The service had already started, and the organist was playing the prelude. I'm not sure they timed his arrival that way, but as soon as we entered the auditorium, the people in the front stood and began clapping. Soon the entire congregation was on their feet. They clapped loudly and for what seemed like a long time.

The kids told me later that's when I started crying. They're probably right, because that would be typical of me, but I wasn't aware of my tears. I stared in shock because I hadn't expected such a response. The building was nearly full, and the people's thunderous applause gave me an overpowering sense of thankfulness. I felt awed by their expressions of kindness and support.

I pushed Don to the front pew, and we sat down. The applause finally stopped and the congregation began their opening hymn. One of the deacons came over and bent down next to Don.

"We would like you to say something."

I could tell by the shock on Don's face that he hadn't thought about saying anything. He nodded in agreement.

"As soon as we finish this song," the deacon said.

After the hymn was over, I wheeled Don up to the front and turned him around so he faced the congregation. I stared at Chris, Joe, and Nicole to see how they were handling it. Nicole is like her mother, and tears had filled her eyes. Both boys were smiling.

The same deacon handed Don the microphone and the applause started again. It reminded me of the wave we often see in the football stands. The wave began on our side of the building and swept across the room. Our friends clapped and clapped. This time it was louder and even more enthusiastic than when we first entered the building. A number of people had tears in their eyes. Almost everyone was smiling.

As I watched and listened, I thought, *This must be a tiny taste of the joy in heaven.* By then I had tears flowing down my cheeks. I smiled and nodded, and was thankful no one asked me to say anything.

Once the people stopped clapping and sat down, Don said exactly four words. I'll never forget and neither will he.

"You prayed; I'm here."

He handed the microphone back to the deacon. I was so proud of Don for those few-but-eloquent words. I knew he believed then, as he does today, that he's alive because God's people prayed for him—especially those at South Park.

I patted Don on the shoulder. It was a small gesture to affirm to him how well he'd spoken. I wheeled him back to the front pew.

As soon as we were back in the front row, I looked at him. He was worn-out, even though he probably wouldn't have said so. He slumped slightly, and I could read the exhaustion on his body as well as his face.

I tried to think of the best way to get out of there. Without saying anything to Don, I motioned for the deacon to come over. "Don needs to go home. This has been too much for him."

"I understand," he said and signaled the "moving crew" to help us.

"He's worn out; he needs to go home," I said as the crew came around to help. They led us down a hallway and out the side door to the van.

From the time he handed back the microphone until we were home again, Don never said another word. I assumed he didn't have the stamina to stay through the entire service. If we had stayed, that would have been only the beginning because he would have had to smile, shake hands, and talk. Most of the people would naturally have insisted on saying something. That really would have exhausted him.

I'd had mixed feelings about Don going back to church after only a few weeks at home. I had sensed he wasn't well enough. Even so, it was a powerful experience for him and for all of us. *But it cost Don.* Afterward, he realized he probably shouldn't have gone and that it was too early.

Once the deacons got him into the house, they helped me put him back into the hospital bed. He was so tired he went to sleep almost immediately.

In those days he slept a great deal. He was recovering from a terrible experience, and he used all the energy he had when he was awake.

I understood, but it didn't make it any easier.

Nicole turned thirteen in June of 1989, less than a month after Don came home. We both wanted her birthday to be special, and not only because she was moving into her teen years. Her birthday would also be an opportunity for us to show that the accident wasn't going to be a permanent disruption to our family.

Although our home didn't have a swimming pool, Nicole had always wanted to have a pool party for her birthday. Several of her friends had pools in their backyards, and it was "the thing" in those days. We were able to rent the public pool because one of the coaches from my school ran it during the summer. He also volunteered to serve as lifeguard so we didn't have that additional expense. We let Nicole make out the guest list and decide what food she wanted.

The event turned out beautifully. We grilled, the girls swam, and then Nicole opened presents. Everything went as planned, and I said to Don, "It was a perfect evening."

As years passed Nicole has forgotten the details, and so have I; but I'll long remember the feeling of being able to plan and hold the party. It was more than a birthday party for our daughter. That's when I knew—truly knew—things were going to be okay.

Planning and holding a birthday party are simple, ordinary occurrences in the lives of many families. For our family nothing had been simple or ordinary for many months. We would never take such things for granted again.

The light was dawning.

⸻

Don lost a lot of weight after the accident. He didn't eat much in the hospital, and he had little to no appetite after we brought him home. No matter what I suggested for a meal or what I cooked, nothing appealed to him. I had to beg him to keep trying, even when he'd say, "I'm not hungry."

Don's doctor's impressed on me the need to get more calories into

Don. The body needs calories to heal, and he wasn't getting what he needed. Of course, to me, as to many wives in my position, his failure to eat also indicated that I had failed. That wasn't true; but that's part of what I struggled with.

Why couldn't I push him to try harder? I coaxed and pleaded, but my words had little effect. It may have been slightly devious—I like to think of it as being creative—but sometimes I would get the kids to help. They would fix a sandwich and bring it to him. It was harder for him to turn them down, especially when they would stand there and ask, "Do you like it, Dad?"

Each time Don ate a little more of his food, it gave us a sense of victory. I felt like a bully or a nag, but I kept at him to eat. As he forced himself to eat more, his appetite improved. Over the summer, he made significant strides. That was one more sign to me that he was getting better.

I recorded in my diary: "Don was cranky today. He's questioning some of my decisions so that must mean he's getting better. He no longer turns away from me or stares into space. He has begun to talk to me."

27.

THE LEARNING CONTINUES

Even though we were home, that didn't mean the health care ended. The visiting nurse came daily for two months. During that same period, a physical therapist visited three times a week.

Don was home, and that brought us closer to normal living again. Physically he was making progress. Emotionally, he still had trouble, and I did as well. After more than fifteen years of being married, we had to shift our roles in the relationship.

I was no longer simply Don's wife and the children's mother. Circumstances had forced me into the position of making all the big decisions. In some ways, that was a more serious walk in darkness than the accident and the first weeks of his recovery. In those days, at least, I could grab the hands of my friends, talk to the medical staff, or find someone to help me make decisions.

How do I make decisions now?

There was no expert to show me how to respond. No handbook, no template. Until the accident I'd never taken care of paying bills—it was something Don liked to do, and I was content to let him. Now I had to pay the bills and make sure we had the money to pay them. With statements and invoices coming, I had to learn to keep our finances straight.

I felt like someone who had gone from working in the mailroom in a giant corporation to being the president, with no training in between. I had to learn to fill out insurance forms, and I had gotten good at doing that. I had to—they were constantly being thrown at me, and Don couldn't do it.

That left only me. And I felt inadequate.

How did I turn things around to make decisions for Don? We think differently about many things, and that's normal. I also knew that some of my decisions might displease him. Because he had been in charge through the previous years of our marriage, it had been hard for me to accept and take over that role. Instead of Don saying to me, "You need to . . ." I was the one saying those words to him. Each time I made another decision, it became easier to make the next one.

In many ways I also took on the role of Don's mother—a mom's caregiving role. After having most of his decisions made for him at the hospital, it was hard for Don to think about and decide anything.

I learned on the job—partially out of necessity—but I became quite good at making decisions. To my surprise I discovered I could evaluate well the different sides of an issue and come to the best decision. A year earlier I wouldn't have seen myself doing that.

I'm not saying it was easy, or that I woke up the day after the accident with new decision-making superpower. It was a growing process. At times I was successful, and on other occasions I was positive I had failed. I had to learn to live by the words I'd often said to my students. "It's okay to make mistakes as long as you learn something from them." I made many mistakes, but each time I tried to learn a lesson so the next time I could make a better choice.

The first real growth achievement after the hospital involved buying another vehicle. Don's car had been totaled in the accident, and the insurance sent us a check for the replacement. The money wasn't enough for a new car, but it was enough for a down payment.

Don wasn't able to choose and buy a vehicle, so that left it up to me. I couldn't buy just any car because it would be a long time before he could drive again. The more I thought and prayed about it, the more it seemed that a van provided the immediate, sensible solution. We could get him and his wheelchair inside.

I've never bought a car before. How do I do it?

I fretted about the idea for a day or so. I'd heard my dad and Don talk about how they talked the salesperson down to the price they would accept when buying a car. Once again my characteristic anti-confrontational side kicked in. *How am I supposed to do that? How can I bargain for a better price?*

Although as a kid I had often helped my dad work on our family cars, could change a tire by myself, and knew a little car language, I had no idea what made a car good or how much was too expensive. In those days there was no Internet to research, and I'm not sure I would have known what to look for even if it had been available.

I also have to admit that my ego was involved. I wanted to impress Don by coming home with the best vehicle, one that would please him because it would be exactly what he would have picked out himself.

Ken, the husband of our insurance agent, Ann Dillman, volunteered to go with me to look at vans. He was quite knowledgeable, so he was able to guide me in terms of price, style, and quality. He knew how to ask the right questions and wouldn't let me get into a bad deal.

Ken didn't take over the process. He let me ask questions and would follow up if needed. I think he understood how important it was for me to feel I'd made the deal. It was such a relief to go with Ken and know he was looking out for me.

After three days of looking, we found a van I liked at the Ford dealer. Ken assured me that it was a good price. It was a new 1989 blue and silver Aerostar.

I liked the level of the seats because they were neither too low nor too high for Don to get into and out of the van. He could stand from his wheelchair, turn, and sit while someone lifted his leg. Then he could slide sideways across the middle seat so the leg was supported.

Later we figured out that we could fold down the middle and back seats to create a full bed. That way Don could face forward and the seats would be under his legs to support him.

I bought the Aerostar because I felt it was exactly what we needed even though I never did like the vehicle very much. It accomplished what we needed it for—transporting Don until he had the fixator taken off his leg.

I was proud of myself for making such a big decision as buying the van and signing the contract. I'm not sure why, but I didn't tell Don what I was going to do. Perhaps it was because I expected him to give me a long list of the things to watch for.

On some level I wanted to prove to myself I could do it, that I could be independent if there ever came a time Don wasn't there. During all the life-threatening crises, I hadn't allowed my brain to focus on Don dying. I was utterly determined to do whatever it took to help him survive. Looking back, I realize that what I'd really needed was to face the truth of how close I had come to losing him. It took me a while, but I finally did just that. I also faced the realization that it could happen again. It was a strong message that one day I might have to go on alone.

After I made the deal and arranged a time to pick up the van, I told Don, "I bought us a second vehicle—a van that will work well for you. I'm going to take the kids to pick it up." I described it and how much Ken had helped me in choosing it.

I don't remember his words, but the look on his face asked, "You did *what*?"

I smiled, hugged him, and left the room before he could question me.

When we picked up the van, the salesman took a picture of the children and me outside our new van and printed the picture on a calendar as a promo for the Ford agency. We kept that calendar on the refrigerator for a long time. It was one of those calendars with a single picture, and the months were attached, to be torn off one by one. For the rest of that year, each time I looked at that picture, I had a sense of pride for what I had done.

It was a fun trip for the kids and me to pick up the van. And it was a first-time experience for me. I finally understood what people meant when they talked about "that new car smell." I inhaled the aroma for days.

The dealer also gave me a package with a number of extras. We drove through a special, free car wash and had certificates for six more. To me it was almost like winning the lottery.

I was proud of myself because I had accomplished what I considered a huge task and had done it without having to ask for Don's help. Because I hadn't done things like that before, I had started my walk in the dark with no confidence in my ability. Each time I made a decision, and especially when deciding to buy the van, I elevated my self-confidence, and my steps felt more secure. I had to develop that confidence level to be able to take over all the responsibilities in the house. I paid bills, balanced the checkbook, dealt with insurance companies, filed legal papers—and that was in addition to being a mother, taking care of a home, buying groceries, and cooking meals.

The day came, of course, when Don was healthy and well enough to resume his role. I had wanted him to do that, but when it came time to hand things over to him, it wasn't easy for me to go back to my former role of letting him make the major decisions alone. I realized how important it was for both of us to have a clear understanding of our household finances.

Before the accident I had relinquished many responsibilities to him because I wasn't interested. He had tried to involve me, with little success. The accident pushed me into unknown territory. During those days I had no choice but to take control.

It was time for Don and me to create a new, working partnership, one in which both of us were involved in making decisions. I found it easier to make that choice than to put it into practice. I understood how it felt to be elevated to an interim position in a company for a few months and having authority to make decisions. After a short period, however, it's back to the old job and loss of authority. That part was difficult for me, and it was hard to let go. I'd been in control and made most of the decisions for more than four months. Sometimes Don asked questions, and he didn't agree with what I had done, but they were my decisions and he accepted them.

One time, when he made it clear that he didn't like what I had done on a particular matter, I said, "I've done this on my own for four months. I've learned to make decisions, and I think I was right on this one." I don't remember which way the conversation went after that, but I do know it was the first time I made the effort to be involved, and that allowed us to really discuss a decision, listen to each other's viewpoint, and come to an understanding. It was a new way of doing things for both of us.

Until the accident I hadn't been the driving force in our family. Then circumstances pushed me into taking over that role. Not only that, but I realized I was actually good at making decisions and handling responsibilities. But for us to reestablish the former balance in our marriage, I would have to turn the authority back to him, and I wasn't ready to do that. I liked my new freedom, and the lessons hadn't been easy to learn. I realized I could never go back and be the mostly silent partner in our decisions.

We both made adjustments over the next few weeks. Neither of us is quite who we were before the accident. Over the years, we've made more adjustments, and our relationship has become a matter of sharing.

The experience has also made me more open and involved. I developed confidence in my ability, even with things I have never faced before. I've discovered I like tackling new problems, researching, and narrowing the choices.

These days, I often do the legwork before Don and I discuss the issue and come to a final resolution. For example, when we made the decision to relocate, I contacted the Realtor, previewed homes, and narrowed the field. We worked together to make the decision.

While I was writing this book, I realized that I probably know more about the details of our finances than Don does. Although it would be years before Don would earn his living as a public speaker instead of a pastor, I was balancing our checking account. Because I stepped in and held on to what I learned, we were ready for me to take care of the business end when Don started going on the road. Since the publication of *90 Minutes in Heaven* in 2004, Don has been on the road constantly. He speaks at least two hundred times a year. When he's home, he needs to rest and recharge. I do as much as I can so he doesn't have to cope with minor problems. And I still enjoy the tasks.

I also want to point out that Don had more confidence in my ability to do those things than I did. Occasionally, especially after he was better, I would ask him to do a task. He didn't refuse, but he didn't do it either.

For example, one time the van needed the oil changed, so I asked him to drive it to have it taken care of because he was able to do that. I don't recall that he said anything, but he certainly didn't say he would.

After the third time I asked, and he still didn't take care of the van, I felt I was nagging, and decided not to ask again. Later that day I got in the van myself and drove it to the mechanic, went through the process, and drove home. I told him what I'd done.

"I knew you could do it." Then he smiled.

That's when I realized he had silently forced me to take another step on my own. I smiled back at him.

He continued to nudge me, but the accident had shoved me to where I learned to become more assertive. I have a stronger sense of who I am and appreciate the things I can do.

Most of all, I've learned to stand up for myself. I can say that I'm not afraid or hesitant to stand up for something if I believe it's important. As I had reminded myself in the hospital, I was stronger. Philippians 4:13 was one of those verses that encouraged me and kept me focused: "I can do everything through Christ, who gives me strength."

I took that verse to heart, and I'm a more assertive person today. I stand up for myself better. I'm not afraid to keep on about something until I get what I need. But I often tell wives, "Your husband doesn't have to get hit by a big truck to learn these truths."

28.
TRAVELING WITH THE YOUTH

Don wanted to get back to work, but he wasn't able to resume his full responsibilities. He was still the youth minister at the South Park Baptist Church in Alvin. *The* big event of the year for young people was youth camp. He obviously couldn't go the summer of 1989.

I'm not sure how it came about, but the leaders in the church selected me to chaperone the youth in his place. I secretly think it was Suzan's idea and Don agreed. It was a conspiracy to get me out of the house.

When we initially talked about my going with the youth, I wasn't enthusiastic. "The last thing I want this summer is to have to spend time with a bunch of teenagers," I said. "I like elementary kids."

Don didn't argue, but he didn't promise to make other arrangements with the church.

The more I thought about it, however, the more open I became. I also realized that I'd have a chance to be with Nicole and her friends because they would ride in our van. I agreed, but still with some hesitation.

Don's mother came to Alvin to stay with him while I went with the kids to Baylor University, in Waco, which was nearly two hundred miles away. The boys stayed at home, and I knew they wouldn't be any problem (they weren't). It would be the first time Nicole was old enough to go with the youth to camp. That was a big event for her.

We left early Monday morning and returned late Friday night. I drove our van loaded with six girls.

We stayed in a dorm. I smiled when I saw the room. It was nicer than what I had slept in at St. Luke's Hospital. I don't remember much except that it was a typical dorm room with twin beds. Each room had built-in desks and shelves. I stayed on the first floor, and we had large windows that faced a street. My roommate, a chaperone from another church, was someone I hadn't known before camp. We were instantly comfortable with each other and ended up spending a lot of time together.

Although the weather was unseasonably hot, we had a delightful time at Baylor. The idea of the youth camp is to strengthen teens and help them grow in their Christian faith. Even though all of us came from Baptist churches in Texas, some of the kids weren't church members, and others hadn't made commitments to Jesus Christ. Camp was also a way to do evangelism by inviting youth who weren't active but were willing to have fun for a few days.

We had Bible studies each morning, sports activities in the afternoons, and a worship service each night. Every event was youth oriented. By the end of the first worship service, I praised God for giving me the opportunity to come, even though I had been reluctant at first.

I didn't worry about Don or the boys all week. I thought about them every day, many times a day, but it was a blessed relief for me to get away for a few days and into something different from my normal routine.

Because Don's mother was handling everything, I was at peace, knowing she would call if they needed me. We didn't have cell phones in those days, so there wasn't any instant checking in. They had the telephone number of the camp, and someone would get the word to me if necessary. (They never called.)

By the time we were ready to return to Alvin, I thanked God for giving me the privilege of being with those teens. I had been uplifted and felt humbled and grateful for the opportunity to serve God by chaperoning those young people.

Each day was special, but the highlight for me took place inside the van on the way back. We were riding along and talking about the events. The girls were excited and buzzing about everything that happened to them during the week.

When there was a pause in the conversation, one girl, who wasn't a member of our church, asked, "What does it mean to be a Christian?"

For me and for the girls, it was exactly the question we wanted to answer. "Rather than trying to answer you while I'm driving," I said, "would you mind if we pulled over to the side of the road and parked? That way I can give you my full attention."

"All right."

I could tell by the way she answered that it was a serious question for her.

I pulled onto the shoulder. I didn't have to say anything to the other girls. There was complete silence for several minutes. Nicole and those sitting close to me had closed their eyes and were praying.

I talked to the girl about God's love and why we need Jesus Christ in our lives. When I paused, two or three teens made helpful comments, and I appreciated that. Not only did they show they understood and wanted her to experience a relationship with the Savior, but I think it made them aware that they were involved in showing their friend the way to follow Jesus Christ.

After perhaps ten minutes she said she understood everything we'd told her. Then she asked the big question: "How do I become a Christian?"

We explained that if she believed—truly believed—that's all God required. Of course, I also talked to her about growing as a believer by reading the Bible and associating with other Christians.

She took in everything I said, and I asked her to pray for God to come into her life. I started with a simple prayer: "Lord, we have a young lady here who wants to come into your kingdom, so she's going to talk to you now."

She bowed her head and said, "Jesus, forgive me of my sins. I want you to come into my heart and to save me."

Two of the girls also prayed for her. Tears flowed. It was such a special time, and everyone seemed excited and delighted for her.

I pulled back onto the road, and the excitement continued all the way back to Alvin.

Later I realized what a blessing I would have missed if I hadn't been at that camp. It's a solemn thought to realize I'd played a role in where that young girl will spend eternity. Without Don's accident, I wouldn't have driven the van that week. It reminds me that God can take an awful situation and use it to shine his light. That day, one young girl's face shone with the light of God's love.

29.

LEARNING TO WALK

Back in Alvin after youth camp, our lives took on a routine. As much as possible, I tried to keep everything moving normally. Having the summer away from the classroom was delightful for me. I had one major task until school started again, and that was to focus on my family.

The summer of 1989 was particularly challenging for us, even with the help of our friends. One of the big things was Don's physical therapy. It still hurt when the therapist worked on him, and he was exhausted afterward.

The physical therapist helped Don out of bed, and the routine began. As soon as Don was able, the therapist helped him stand and start walking. Don didn't refuse, but he didn't want to do all the things demanded of him. He did everything his therapists asked, but he moaned and at times griped about it later and threatened not to comply the next time.

It was a daily battle. It was hard on me watching him fight through the therapy. Many times as I stared at his face while he writhed in pain, I wanted to say to the therapist, "Stop! He's had enough." I didn't, of course, because Don had to endure the pain to get better. Those were the times I had to think about the future. Without the therapy Don would never regain the ability to walk. It was a price worth paying, on both our parts. Many times I had to leave the room so he would not see me cry. I hurt because he hurt.

Don still wore the device on his leg, but the therapist felt it was important to use the muscles he still had. The fixator stayed on his arm until May, fewer than five months after the accident. After it was removed, we procured a walker, and Don learned to walk with it. The rental house had a patio at the back where he could practice.

———

Our lives grew more complicated. By the middle of summer, we were back in church, including Don, although he was in a wheelchair with the fixator on his leg.

Many folks think ministers work only on Sunday. I have a truth to announce. Ministers are on call twenty-four hours a day, seven days a week. It is a demanding profession, and Don has always given unselfishly of his time and energy to his calling. The summer is filled with more activities than usual because it's the busiest time of year for youth.

Don didn't want his group to miss anything. In between physical therapy and doctors' visits (which required an hour's travel time both to and from the medical center), I tried to pitch in and help whenever I could. I also wanted to reestablish some normalcy for our children. Two eight-year-old boys and a teenage girl can come up with lots of things they want to do.

For months my primary focus was acting as caregiver for Don as well as being mom to three kids. Although it was demanding to take care of the children and a still physically dependent husband, I was happy to do it. As the summer wore on, I became better equipped to juggle the activities. I was still paying the bills, taking care of legal issues, and keeping a watchful eye on Don to make sure he didn't overdo it. (I had to hold him back several times.)

When my students at school struggled with math or spelling words, I often said, "Stay at it. The more you do something, the better you get." That's the way I felt about all that I had to do.

At times I wasn't successful at juggling all the activities at the same time. A few times I scheduled two things at once or didn't leave enough time between events. (Most people were understanding and forgiving.) But within a few weeks, I became comfortable in my new role of commander in chief of the Piper family. Others helped, and I appreciated their doing that, but I had the responsibility of making sure everything ran smoothly.

One significant and ongoing task during the summer was cleaning the pinholes in Don's fixator. As I mentioned earlier, someone had to clean them every day, and I chose to do it. The biggest problem was keeping his skin from adhering to the wires. Initially we used pieces of gauze soaked in Hibiclens, a disinfecting soap, with one side cut to fit around the wire. While cutting the slit didn't take a long time, I had to be careful no threads were loose to get tangled in the wires or his skin.

As always, medical technology moves forward. I learned that an improved method had been invented. To teach me, a nurse brought in a box of the new material. Inside were a hundred little circles of foam rubber, each with a slit cut into one side. A small plastic screw held it in place around the wire. The foam would soak in the Hibiclens and then be put around the wire.

One time I looked at the small box, and the price tag was still on it. Each box contained one hundred discs, and each disc cost $6.60—that meant a box of one hundred cost $660. We used three dozen discs a day. That was one more reminder of the costs building up for Don's hospitalization.

He also had to receive shots, primarily for pain and antibiotics. I learned to inject him as well. Within a few days after moving in, our den looked like a hospital room. But it lifted Don's spirits to be home.

On the second day in the house, he looked out the window and said, "I can see people who don't wear white uniforms."

Having him home was certainly more work for me, but it was worth it. Each day, I felt our lives were slowly returning to some form of normal—not the kind we had known before, but an adjusted normal. Don was still depressed, but it wasn't as bad as it had been in the hospital.

Don had spent 105 days in the hospital, but now he was home. For a total of thirteen months he would lie in a hospital bed. But except for a few relapses, he improved each day.

He began to walk again, even with the thirty-pound, stainless-steel ring on his left leg. The first day he tried, he took exactly three steps and nearly collapsed.

Don thought he had failed; I rejoiced because he had succeeded. I was delighted that he was actually walking on his own.

Three steps doesn't sound like much, but for someone who hadn't walked for nearly four months and who had been told he would never walk again, even three steps was an amazing achievement. It's like when your child takes his first step. I thought about parents of young children. "Our baby took her first step today," they say, and beam with pride. They get excited about the smallest progress. I fondly remembered how we felt with all three of our children. I knew only too well where Don started and how far he had come to accomplish the act of walking.

As I watched his progress, I was so proud of Don. I wanted to call everyone and share my excitement. Each person I talked to rejoiced with me. Their enthusiasm added to my joy.

After his initial three steps, Don improved a little each day. Within the next couple of months, despite having that horrible device on his leg, he was walking around the house—but not gracefully or quickly. I smiled as I watched him hobble around. He looked funny, but he *was* walking.

———

It was a relief to know we didn't have to worry about paying the medical bills, but Don did have to go to a hearing one time. Though our lawyer took care of everything, Don still had to appear in person for a deposition in the fall of 1989. He had to go to court so the Worker's Compensation committee could see him and prove what he claimed. I didn't attend because I was teaching, so our lawyer picked Don up and took him to downtown Houston.

Workers' Compensation has their own facility on Tuam Street in downtown Houston. Upon arrival there, our lawyer wheeled Don into the room. Several members of the board sat at a large round table up front.

When Don's turn came—he was still wearing the fixator—they stared at him and his hideous device. The head of the committee said, "We don't need you to say anything, Mr. Piper. We're going to take care of this. We're sorry we made you come today. We had no idea you were so badly injured."

His condition was evident, and seeing him in person was all they needed. It was obvious that Don deserved whatever compensation they could give him. Workers' compensation has never been a problem since then. He has lifelong medical benefits for anything relating to the accident.

The only problem we might face is that if anything should come up that's not listed in the initial accident report—even though it's a complication from it—we have to fight for coverage. We frequently have to go through several steps to prove it's a problem related to the accident. There is usually a battle between our workers' compensation insurance and our regular health insurance. Neither wants to pay, and each claims it's the other's responsibility. I've spent hours on the phone getting it straightened out.

A few times I've had to say firmly, "I don't care who pays for it. I just want my husband taken care of. To whom do I need to speak in order for that to happen?"

That brings results. Some of the lessons I learned from the accident I still use.

Don had been home from the hospital for a short time and was still in bad shape, but he was improving, which was what mattered most. That's when we learned that Nicole had earned the rank of Queen with a Scepter in a coronation ceremony at South Park Baptist Church.

She was part of a Southern Baptist organization called Girls in Action (or GA) for younger girls and Acteens for junior high and high school girls. She fulfilled all the requirements to be eligible for the honor, which included a high level of activity, such as memorizing a certain number of Bible verses, doing projects, and participating in mission trips.

Most of the time she fulfilled the requirements while she was boarding with Stan and Suzan Mauldin. I tried to encourage her when I could; Don was too ill to be much aware of what she was going through.

That meant Nicole did it on her own without prompting from either of us. When we learned of her honor, it made us even more proud of her.

It also created a problem. One of the traditions of the coronation was that the father escorted the queen down the aisle.

To our delight, Don's doctors discharged him from the hospital shortly before the coronation ceremony. I didn't think it was a good idea for him to venture out so soon, but it was important to Don. As he said, "It isn't her wedding, but it is the biggest moment in her young life."

Don, still in his wheelchair, went with her. Nicole held his arm as he rolled down the aisle. The twins, carrying the crown and scepter on pillows, walked behind them. The boys also rolled the wheelchair because Don was unable to do that for himself since his left arm had been so badly injured.

The evening was special to us. Despite his pain, Don beamed in a way I hadn't seen since the accident. The smile on Nicole's face made it clear that she felt honored to have her father "walk" down the aisle with her.

I stayed in the back and watched as tears rolled down my cheeks. A few others in the South Park audience cried as well. It was quite an emotional moment. Most of the people were impressed that Don was there, but the evening belonged to Nicole.

By the time we brought Don home that night, he was exhausted— as I knew he would be. His pain level shot up from the exertion, but he didn't complain. Being with his daughter in her first major event was worth the pain.

———

In late August or early September, Don came outside while I was washing the van. He wasn't through with his wheelchair, but he could walk short distances either with his walker or his crutches. He came out the front of the house and watched. We were chatting about nothing important.

I stopped to empty the bucket of dirty water. I was almost finished and became absorbed in cleaning up.

Chris came around and said, "Dad wanted the car keys."

I turned around. Don was sitting in the front seat of the van— on the driver's side—he held the keys in his right hand, smiled, and jingled them.

"What are you doing?" I asked. He still wore that Ilizarov fixator on his leg.

"I'm going to drive."

"No, you're not," I started to argue. "It's too early for—" And then I saw his expression. "Okay."

I didn't think Don was ready to drive, but the determination on his face and the way he held himself made me realize it wasn't a matter for discussion. It was one of those times when he knew what he wanted to do. Nothing was going to stop him from trying.

I hadn't seen that determination on his face since the accident.

Although I considered it too soon, his emotional state was more important.

Don cranked the engine while I closed the passenger side door. I stood on the driveway as he slowly backed the van into the street. It took everything I had not to jump in front of the van so he couldn't drive forward. In my head I understood his need to get back into the driver's seat, but my heart screamed no.

Until that moment, even when I wasn't with Don, I knew he was dependent on others to care for him and provide for his needs. His driving meant that for the first time since the accident, he was on his own.

As he turned the corner, I prayed for God to keep him safe. Since the accident I had had more practice with letting go of my fears and giving them to God. That's not to say I didn't ever worry, but I had reached a point where I didn't allow fear to control me.

Don was gone only a few minutes as he drove around the block, although it seemed like a long, long time. I didn't breathe easy until the van turned back onto our street.

When he drove back into the driveway, the look of triumph on his face was amazing. It was as if he had said, "I have some control over my life now. I can drive. I can do things."

His driving that day was a strong statement of independence.

After that drive it was as if Don had passed his first driving test. He drove pretty much everywhere. We climbed into the van and he drove us to the mall a short distance from our house. When he got out of the van, most of the time we helped him get into his wheelchair. Walking with the device on his leg was still problematic, and the pull of gravity made it worse. The kids and I took turns pushing Don as we walked around the mall. People often stared as we passed by because Don's device brought us a lot of unwanted attention.

That provided yet another lesson for me and our children. Today we are sensitive to those dealing with handicapping conditions. We remember how it felt to be seen as some type of freak show. Even with the unwanted stares and occasional comments, we enjoyed spending time together and being a family.

This was progress, and it made such a difference in Don's attitude. He was mobile again and wasn't stuck inside the house all the time.

As hard as he tried to get well, Don still had little stamina, and it didn't take much to wear him out. It wasn't only the lack of stamina, but his weight was still down. He was beginning to put on pounds, but not many. Some of his muscles had atrophied because they hadn't been used, although the twice-weekly therapy sessions did help to rebuild the muscle mass.

One of the things we did was make him protein shakes every day. We experimented with different flavors, trying to find one he would enjoy and drink. His favorite turned out to be banana. All of this was part of the therapy and diet process. It still took months before he could return to doing normal things for sustained periods of time.

I continued to think of that drive around the block. That was *the* moment of change. The determination in his face shouted, "I'm going to do this!" After that drive he was different. He improved on a number of levels.

"I'm getting my husband back," I said to myself. I knew even then and saw it more clearly later, however, that the pre-accident Don was gone.

I was saddened by the thought that Don would no longer be the daredevil he had once been. Waterskiing with the youth even though he couldn't swim, going down a black-diamond slope on his first snow skiing trip—which he assured me was by accident; I'm not convinced—those were things he wouldn't do again. Don loved to play tennis, to walk, to ride bikes. Those things, too, were in his past. I hurt for his loss of them.

But Don the man was coming back. I could see on his face a new strength, a sense of purpose, and especially hope. He would never be the same, but he was definitely closer to being who he had been before the accident than he had been for the previous months.

30.
GOOD-BYE TO THE FIXATOR

November of 1989 remains a special time for Don and me for one important reason: the Ilizarov apparatus had done its work, and he was ready for his doctor to remove it. If the device had worked successfully—and we weren't positive it had—Don could start to walk on his own. We were both excited and a little anxious for the event.

I took the day off from school and drove Don to St. Luke's Hospital. We were both tense; I felt as if we held our breaths the entire trip. Dr. Tom Greider removed the device (we still have part of it to show people). Then he put a walking brace on Don's leg. Because he had been with us through most of Don's ordeal, we were on a first-name basis with Tom.

As I recall, it took about six hours for him to take off that steel cage. After he'd removed it, he came into the waiting room with a huge smile on his face.

That was enough for me, but he added, "Eva, it went very well."

I felt relieved, even though I hadn't expected anything to go wrong. Yet to hear him say so enabled me to relax.

Tom sat down next to me and said, "There is one thing. When the bones healed, one slid up over the other."

"And what does that mean?"

"The bones don't match evenly. Don will be a little shorter on his left side."

"How much shorter?"

"About an inch and a half," he said. "But the procedure worked. It knitted and did exactly what it was supposed to do. I put metal plates along the inside of his leg to stabilize the bone. Eventually we'll be able to remove the plates when the bone strengthens."

Tom was proud of his work—as he should have been. It was a new medical procedure and I think the first anyone had ever done on a femur in this country. I realized then that he hadn't been quite as confident in the beginning as he had appeared.

"The Ilizarov did what it was supposed to do," he repeated. "It wasn't perfect. The daily turning of the screws pulled the bones together. If it had gone perfectly, the two bones would have met exactly and both of his legs would now be the same length. But somewhere during the growth of the bone, the top bone slipped a little over the bottom."

Despite the lack of perfection, the Ilizarov frame had functioned as it was supposed to, and Don had kept his leg. That in itself was a miracle.

———

For the removal of the fixator, Don had to be put to sleep. It was a long process. After the staff took him from the recovery room, they sent him to a hospital room. I was waiting there when the door opened and his gurney was brought in. He was covered with a sheet. Previously, the sheet had covered that huge fixator device, creating a kind of tent. This time it was different. The sheet actually covered his leg. It was the first time anything had touched the skin on his leg for ten months! Tears of joy sprang to my eyes.

That sounds like a small thing, but that was an image I can still see in my mind. He had come through those months of agony and would soon walk on his own legs.

His left leg was swollen, of course, and wrapped in an ACE bandage, but the device was gone. That made it a special day for me.

The brace Don had to wear was made of leather and metal. The leather belt strapped around his waist, and flat metal bars went down the length of his leg. A black shoe was attached to the new device. The brace kept his left leg straight to support it so that the bone could continue to heal. It would be many months before he could remove this leg brace. The device kept him from bending it for the moment; the doctors weren't sure what kind of bend he would be able to have in his leg later.

The pins were gone, and the wires no longer went through his legs. He would be more mobile. Before that day ended, he was able to walk a few steps on crutches. Because he didn't have to carry the extra weight of the Ilizarov, walking was easier.

We smiled at each other as we ambled down the hallway.

We still weren't ready to dispose of the wheelchair, but it received less and less use. If Don stayed up too long or overtired himself, he used his crutches or his walker. On a few occasions, he was so exhausted he dropped into the wheelchair.

The occasional use of the wheelchair didn't discourage Don or me. The physical therapy was paying off, and his condition was improving.

Don's stamina increased, and it seemed that I could see it improving day by day. Some days, however, he overdid it, and the next day he'd be back in the wheelchair. But that was all right. The back-and-forth process became part of our new lifestyle. When we used the wheelchair, I became an expert in helping him. I could push him anywhere and get him over curbs and holes. At one point I thought, *Our life is filled with wheelchairs, crutches, walkers, and braces, but it's still a good life. Don and I are together.*

It was good. His depression was all but gone, and I felt I had my husband back again. Don would never be physically the same. In many ways we both had been changed emotionally by the accident. We had settled into a new way of life. Don began to regain his confidence and his drive. Underneath all the hardware he was still the man I loved and married.

31.

THE MANY QUESTIONS

Have you ever questioned God or asked why you had to go through this?" As I said in a previous chapter, I hear that question fairly often.

The answer is yes, I have questioned God—a few times. But I'm not sure I ever asked God why we had to go through our ordeal. Truthfully, I accepted it as God's will. Perhaps it's my military upbringing that enables me to accept events without questioning authority. Maybe God gave me a good dose of faith. Either way, most of the time—and I mean *most*—I was fine.

I did question why God allowed this to happen to my husband. "He's a minister and a faithful servant," I'd pray. "We've given up everything for you. We haven't wanted material things or disobeyed you."

I still have no totally satisfactory answer, and yet, in the years since the publication of *90 Minutes in Heaven*, Don has touched millions of lives. He could never have had such a powerful, worldwide ministry if he hadn't gone through the accident. That's as close as I can come to answering my own question.

When Don and I married, I didn't know he would go into the ministry. He was in sales for a TV station and liked his job very much. After he felt God wanted him to be a minister, I accepted it, but he didn't have my full backing. I simply acknowledged that was what God wanted him to do, and I wouldn't want to stand in his way. Maybe I was being a typical woman here, but I wanted a husband and a family, and I yearned to stay in one place and not move every two or three years.

I had gone through that frequent moving as the child of a military man, and now I wanted stability. I wanted us to live in the same city all through our lives together so we could dig deep roots.

My folks moved to Bossier City, Louisiana, when I was a senior in high school. Our time there was the longest I had lived in one place.

Fourteen years after Don and I married, we moved to Texas. When we moved, I did hold some resentment toward God. I had given my life to God, but now, instead of staying in Bossier City where I would have been content, we had moved to Texas, and I had to learn to adjust. It took me a while, but I was able to let go of the resentment.

I want to make all this clear because I'm not a perfect Christian, and I'm not beyond doubting, complaining, and even resenting some of the things God has done. Those negative feelings were temporary, but they were there.

I can usually pause and ponder all the positive things God has done for me and for our family. Even now, I look back at Don's accident and I wish it hadn't happened. Of course I do, but I also see something else: Even in the worst of times, God comes through and makes good come out of those terrible experiences.

Too often people—both within and outside the Christian community—have expectations of the way good or spiritual believers are supposed to behave when bad times come. They expect them to say, "It's all right. It's the will of God."

God isn't surprised by our tragedies, but those bad times don't mean we shrug and say, "Fine. Whatever." We have feelings and aspirations. We question things. God gave us the ability to raise questions and to want to know.

Especially during the first weeks after the accident, I was exhausted on every level: physically, mentally, emotionally, and spiritually. I was often drained and wondered if I could go through the new routine one more time—things such as going to the hospital or living another day without our children at home. I knew I could, but it *felt* as if my tank was on empty and I had used up all my resources. I had to find ways to work through those difficult times. My friends Suzan and Susan probably did more to sustain me than anyone.

Some days were incredibly difficult, and I felt isolated from everyone. That was especially true on the days no one visited us in the hospital. It was a long drive from Alvin to the medical center, and people had their own lives. I understood that, but my emotions lagged behind my reasoning ability.

In my worst moments I truly wished someone would have been there for me, to speak to me, to encourage me and to say, "It's all right, Eva."

That was especially true after the first week following the accident. For the first few days, people seemed to stream into the hospital. It took about a month for the visitor pool to dry up. Each week fewer and fewer came to see us. Of course there were those we could count on being there on a regular basis, but mostly people stopped coming. I understand: life gets in the way.

Now I'm more conscious of being a long-term friend. When I speak in public, I encourage people to mark their calendars or put a reminder on their phones or computers to check in on those they know are in a long-term tough place.

I felt some pity for myself. I had to sit in the hospital room from three until eleven o'clock with no one to talk to except the nurse, on occasion. Don was in the room, but he wasn't talking. I felt pushed out of his life, and it hurt.

A number of times I left the hospital after those hours of sitting alone and feeling alone. I felt defeated, overwhelmed by what I had neglected at school or at home, and inadequate to handle it all.

Even though I write this, I also know those painful times were part of my growth, and on some level I was aware that God would strengthen me through it all. That doesn't mean I liked what I had to learn.

One of the things I learned, and this probably sounds simplistic, was to pray without closing my eyes and bowing my head. I don't recall that anyone ever said there was only one way to pray, but praying with closed eyes was the pattern I'd learned early in childhood. I absorbed those implied teachings and never questioned them. Bowing my head and closing my eyes, we were taught, was the way to avoid distraction.

A liberating truth for me was that I could drive down the highway and spontaneously talk to God. I was alone going to and from the medical center, so I spent much of that time opening my heart to God.

"Thank you, God, that I have friends at school who're helping to share my load."

"You are so wonderful. Thank you for the progress Don has made this week."

"Thank you that the children are cared for and I don't have to worry about them."

"Here's what I'd like you to do for me . . ."

"I'm done in, God. Worn out. I don't think I can do this anymore."

Sometimes my prayer went like this: "Why? Why did you let this happen? Why did you have it in your plan to allow my husband to be hurt like this?" That kind of praying was often accompanied by tears and sometimes beating on the steering wheel in frustration.

Whether the tears were of frustration or happiness, those were some of the most meaningful prayers that I have prayed in my life. God was with me, and I felt a true closeness. It was such a big change for me to speak from my heart and not worry about how it sounded. I was letting go, telling God what was going on—and I felt better.

Once I let go of my emotional restraints, I sensed God's arms around me. I didn't receive any audible answers, but I did receive peace. That's when prayer—true prayer—became a vital part of my life. God was with me and always had been. I knew that, but there was something else: I realized God didn't mind how angry I became. He didn't mind my questioning, my frustration, or my yelling. God could handle anything I gave him.

Several times, I've spoken to people and urged them to pray, and the individuals have responded, "I couldn't talk to God about that."

"Don't you think he already knows? Your feelings aren't a secret from God."

I wouldn't want to undo my prayer experiences inside the car, even though I hated the circumstances. The prayers were liberating. We're the children of God, and God is my Father. Parents want to hear from their children, and certainly that's true with God. If my earthly father loves to hear from me, I know my heavenly Father wants to hear even more.

One of the best things about talking with God is that I don't have to censor or hesitate. He knows already, and it's so freeing to be emotionally naked before God. I didn't always grasp that, but once I understood, it was liberating.

When I trust God enough to let the words and the emotions roll, I know I'm exactly right in our relationship. I'm honest. I care enough and believe enough to face God's closeness and willingness to love me that I hold back nothing.

Prayer is a two-way relationship, even though many people don't treat it that way. Too often we think prayer means we talk, and God listens. As I grow, I also realize that God wants to talk and will continue to speak if I learn to listen. I don't hear a voice, but I sense the voice of God in my soul. I see the evidence of his presence.

God truly answers my prayers, and I have no doubt about that, even though sometimes I get answers I don't like. My sister-in-law died of cancer at age thirty-nine. I prayed—our whole family did— and God answered by saying no to us. My mother died after having a stroke. Those are the kinds of answers I don't like to receive, but they are answers. My faith in a loving God is strong enough that I can face them and say God has a better plan than I do.

Paying attention to my children has helped me to understand the way God works. In their growing up, they often asked for things they didn't need. They wanted things badly—at least at that moment. And I never minded their asking, but I also had to say no to them. Even though it was sometimes difficult to turn them down, I did it because it was the right thing to do.

Because God loves me and wants only the best for me, I can accept no for an answer when I plead for a positive response. As we're going through turmoil and dark places, we can't see what's going on, but God sees clearly even in the darkest moments.

With my children, it would have been a lot easier to throw up my hands for the sake of peace and give them everything they wanted. Some parents seem to feel that if they don't, their kids won't love them or respect them.

I'm convinced it's the other way around. By withholding at the appropriate times, we not only teach our children values about what's significant in life, but we show them that we care enough to say no. We teach them that some things may be desirable, but they're not good for them.

My responsibility as a parent is to look out for their best interests and to be responsible for the decisions I make. Because I'm willing to tell my children no, as a parent on earth, I've learned to accept the fact that sometimes my heavenly Father is going to tell me no. He knows what's ultimately best for me.

———

In another place I pointed out that people occasionally asked how I was doing, and my answer was "Fine." Sometimes I'd say, "It's tough, so please keep us in your prayers that we're going to make it."

I wasn't lying, but I was putting on a face and protecting myself.

I can now admit that I was afraid to open up when they occasionally asked. I was afraid that if I told them how difficult life was for me, I'd lose it—I'd cry and would not be able to pull myself back together again.

It was easier to smile and say, "Fine" or "All right."

When I was a child, I learned the story about the little Dutch boy who put his finger in the dike and kept everything safe. That's a bit how I felt. If I allowed a trickle of my pain or discouragement to come through, I feared the whole dam would break and I'd fall apart.

Don didn't seem to need me in the hospital; I needed to be there, and yet I wondered what good I was doing. I felt many times that Don was getting all the support he needed, but I had no one. I had friends, but I refer to the feelings and not the reality. If I released even a little of my pain or confusion, I feared that I could never get myself back together again.

If I fell apart, who would take care of Don? Who would take care of the kids? My thinking wasn't rational, even though I was able to function on a rational level. I was living on emotional exhaust fumes—barely making it many days.

The best relationships on earth don't focus only on the happy times but on the sharing of what's deep within our hearts. The best relationships are what I call the sticky, down-in-the-dirt times. They may be unpleasant and hard to cope with, but those dark, confusing, and often painful moments are when our relationships grow stronger.

Until the accident I lived on a surface-level relationship with God. Had anyone challenged me and called me shallow, I probably would have been offended, but it's true. I think most people—church people—live on the level I did. That's not to criticize or condemn, only to face the reality.

In the twenty-plus years since the accident, my life and my commitment to Christ have grown richer and fuller. I hate that it took Don's wreck to bring me to that point. I feel guilty because our Savior deserves more than that. I didn't give him that level of commitment for a long time.

When I talk to people these days, I say, "You need to build that relationship between you and God. You have to work at it to make it real. And the big part of that growth comes through your prayer life."

I once said to a friend, "I learn most of my lessons by hardship and failure."

He laughed and said, "No, you learn *all* your lessons by hardship and failure."

That may have been an exaggeration, but it's not far from the truth. When life is easy and soft, there's little incentive to change. When we face the pain in our lives, and especially when those we love are desperate, we become desperate for more of God.

———

For weeks Don still slept in the hospital bed in the den. One special memory stands out for Don and me. Each day after school, Chris rushed in through the front door and lay his head on Don's chest. It was as if he were listening for Don's heart. Chris has always been the more affectionate one.

Joe stood by the bed and said, "Hi, Dad." He wasn't demonstrative like his twin, but the affection was in his eyes and his voice.

By then, Nicole had become a teenager and was becoming more interested in teenage things, which was natural. She stopped to check on her dad, but often the phone would ring, and she'd be off and engaged in girl talk.

The accident made all of us aware of how quickly things change. We had been a close family, and we took it for granted. I could never have imagined that our family would suffer a tragedy or be separated.

Once we were back together, I saw a change in each of us. We took the time to express to one another how much each person meant to us. It's not as if we lived with a black cloud over our heads, but we had a clear understanding that our loved ones could be gone in a matter of moments. It made us all appreciate each other more.

32.

A Trip to Heaven

In Don's book *90 Minutes in Heaven*, he explains how he held on to his sacred secret for several months before finally sharing it with David Gentiles and Cliff McArdle. I was to find out later my husband had made an amazing journey to heaven and back.

Ever since Dick met with me in the hall outside Don's room in Hermann and told me Don had died, I kept asking myself questions. I felt something had happened to Don, but I couldn't process what it might be. In those days my mind had been filled with taking care of him. As time went on, however, occasionally I wondered what happened.

Even though Don hadn't told me, I had an inkling of something significant, and that feeling wouldn't go away—but I had no sense that he'd gone to heaven. A death-to-heaven-and-back-to-life experience was beyond my comprehension.

Something was troubling Don, and I couldn't figure out what it was. I was aware that after all he had endured and his constant pain, his dejected condition made sense. But there was something else. Something deeper. Something he hadn't told me. Something that had happened at the time of the accident.

Something had occurred. I was sure of it, although I didn't voice that to anyone. It would probably have sounded crazy. Perhaps in my own way I was struggling with the same issue Don had—who would believe me?

I had heard people talk about near-death experiences, but I had always been skeptical. They might have happened in Bible times, but did they happen now? Yet I couldn't shake the feeling that Don had experienced something supernatural. I just couldn't put my finger on it.

As I mentioned earlier, in the Bible, the apostle Paul spoke about going into Paradise, which he also called the third heaven, and coming back to earth. Had something like that happened to Don? As strange as that thought was, I couldn't get away from it. I kept thinking and wondering what had happened—what had *really* happened—to Don.

———

More than a year after the accident, I learned what had happened to Don when I overheard him relating his story to J. B. Perkins, an elderly minister and mentor. I was surprised—but not nearly as much as I might have been. Though the conversation shocked me, it confirmed what I'd felt and hadn't been able to put into words.

After J. B. left, I walked into the room, sat down, and said, "When you were dead, did you go to heaven?"

"Yes."

That's all he said. He was worn out after the lengthy conversation with J. B. so I didn't push him for details.

As I sat next to his bed, things made sense to me. *That's why he's been acting this way. Why would anyone want to come back from heaven? Why wouldn't he resent having the pain and being physically limited?*

I want to make it clear: I wasn't hurt that I wasn't the first person to find out. That never bothered me. I felt elated to know because it enabled me to understand the man to whom I was married.

I had grown up in the church, and all my life I'd heard about heaven (and hell). It was something we accepted because it was in the Bible, and we'd heard many sermons on the topic. I never thought of heaven as one of those places with clouds and harps. I was taught and believed that it was a place of mansions and streets made of gold—literally all the things recorded in the book of Revelation. So to me, heaven was real. It wasn't imminent, but it would be the place I went after I died.

Later, after he had rested, Don opened up and told me more about his time in heaven. He told me about the people who met him at the gate. He saw his grandfather, whom he called Papa. As he told me, I remembered that I had been pregnant with the twins when Don got the call about Papa having a heart attack and dying.

Don also told me his grandmother had been there. I had never known her because she died before we married.

For a long time he focused on the aromas and the indescribable colors. The perfect music. His description of the music touched me most. I'm a musician, and I was awed by his description of the sounds in heaven.

That day he didn't go into detail, as he did later, but he told me enough, and I believed every word. It didn't occur to me then or afterward that Don had gone through a near-death experience. I've read many such accounts, and his wasn't anything like theirs. I'm convinced he truly died and was prayed back to earth. Once he'd given me an overview of his experience, I realized how much it had affected him. Even though he didn't have to say so, he added, "It's the best place I've ever been."

———

Don wanted the two of us to get away for a few days. Between Christmas and New Year's—a time when little goes on in the church and I was on Christmas break—we arranged for our children to stay with my parents. Don drove the van all the way to New Orleans. That's about 350 miles, and not once did he ask me to drive.

I didn't ask if he wanted me to take over. This was one more time when the old Don emerged with grit in his expression and determination in his actions. I didn't want to do anything to hinder this next step of improvement. We stopped twice, and he had the stamina for the entire drive. We had a wonderful time enjoying the sights of New Orleans, walking along the Mississippi River, and shopping. I thought about when a year ago we had discussed getting away to the church planning retreat in January. It seemed a lifetime since the pre-wreck part of my life. That's how I see life now: pre-wreck and post-wreck. There were so many things to be thankful for.

The kids were in school, and as far as we could tell, none of them had lost anything in their studies. I had been afraid that the boys being at school in my parents' town may have disrupted their learning, but I saw no evidence of that. Again, I was thankful to God for helping our kids thrive in the midst of our chaotic living.

I had learned to lean on friends and family members, and they had enabled me to go through rough times. I didn't lean on them quite as much after that, but there was a deep, deep assurance that I could call on them if I needed them.

If I learned any special lesson during that year after Don's accident, it was that people want to help, and I had to be open to them and give them permission to do things for us.

My dad wanted Don to talk about the wreck and his recovery at Riverside Baptist Church in Bossier City, the church where my parents worshipped. Dad had heard some of the information about the experience, but Don hadn't talked to him in detail about it.

Dad was able to get Don invited to preach on a Sunday morning at Riverside. Not only were my parents present but our whole family was there, including Don's parents; his maternal grandmother; and my brother, Eddie Pentecost; his wife, Joyce; and their two children.

Don spoke about the wreck, and then he told them about his brief experience in heaven. He focused his message on the biblical passage where Jesus says, "Don't let your hearts be troubled. Trust in God, and trust also in me. There is more than enough room in my father's home. If this were not so, would I have told you that I am going to prepare a place for you?" (John 14:1–2).

We had a good service, and the people were amazed and responded enthusiastically. Afterward we went to my parents' house for lunch.

Dad called Don aside to talk to him. I wasn't privy to the conversation, but this is how I remember what my father told me.

Dad took Don's hand and said, "I owe you an apology."

"Why?"

Tears filled Dad's eyes and he said, "I was angry with you and especially upset about the way you treated Eva and the kids. I couldn't understand why you would do that to them." Dad paused and said, "Today when I heard about heaven, I realized . . ." He began to shake his head slightly, trying to find exactly the right words. "I realized that if you were alive and lying in pain in the hospital, how angry it must have made you to have to come back."

"I was."

"I know that now, son. Can you forgive me?"

"There's nothing to forgive."

Dad smiled, tears in his eyes, and patted Don on the back.

That experience speaks well for where all the adults in our family were. Until they heard him speak that Sunday morning, none of them really understood why he'd acted as he did. Yet once they heard about his going to heaven, all resentment vanished.

No one in the family ever questioned that Don's experience was real; no one even suggested it was one of those near-death experiences. They didn't question it for two reasons. First, they heard it as Don's own account. To hear him talk about what happened is electrifying. He saw no tunnels or bright lights. For him, it was an instantaneous transformation from this earth to heaven.

But the other reason is that we knew Don. He was one of those logical, orderly thinkers. To speak of such an experience would be totally out of character for him. He might have explained the five lessons he learned from the accident; he would not have talked about an experience, especially an emotional one.

I used to get irritated with him and call him Mr. Spock (from *Star Trek*) because everything for him was so logical. I wanted him to be more emotional—to handle his emotions more like I do.

After the accident Don changed. He can still turn on the Mr. Spock personality, but that's rare. He became a man who feels and expresses emotions. He now shares his experiences openly, and none of us doubted his sincerity as he told his story—especially because we remember the old, guarded Don.

———

Don began gradually regaining some of his previous personality traits—although we knew he'd never be physically the same as he had been. But he was alive; he was walking, and he was walking on his own two legs.

Because his left leg is about an inch and a half shorter, it forced his backbone to curve. In the years since the accident, his back often hurts, and so do his hip joints. Our bodies are made to work in a certain way. When something is off, it creates extra pressure on other parts of the body. He also deals with increased arthritis throughout his body. It was something the doctors told me would happen as a result of the trauma sustained in the accident.

He can't straighten his left elbow, even though Dr. Greider operated on it several times. He told me, "Because the elbow was fractured on the inside, when it knitted itself back together, it did it in such a way that I couldn't straighten it out."

———

"Did you ever ask God to totally heal Don?"

I've heard that question many times. I'm not sure what people mean when they ask, but I wonder if it's a veiled accusation meaning, "Wouldn't Don be totally well today if you had prayed for his total healing?" Or are they questioning whether God is powerful enough to completely heal Don? Or are they thinking God is punishing us in some way?

Most often I think they are true questioners who are seeking to understand how God works.

Of course I prayed for his healing. I wanted my pre-crash husband back. And it's not something I stopped asking, even after his thirty-four surgeries.

I pray that way even today. Don continues to struggle with many physical limitations, although people won't hear him complaining. His body is wearing out, and it saddens me to see it happening.

Yes, I prayed. Yes, I still pray. It appears that God isn't going to give Don a whole body in this life. Mostly I pray for pain relief because I see how much he hurts. People who don't know him and have only read about him in his four books are flabbergasted at how well he does.

He looks healthy.

"You don't even walk with a limp," people often say. It's true: he doesn't, but they don't know that it takes an immense amount of self-discipline and effort on his part. Don won't wear lifts in his shoe. The lift would make him feel handicapped, and he refuses to claim that label. Not that he finds that word degrading, which he doesn't, but it's for his own self-image that he shies away from the description.

He walks normally. When he occasionally limps, it's due to the pain of arthritis or because he has overexerted himself. That means he just doesn't have the strength to walk like a healthy person.

Don feels pain every waking moment. Every day of his life there is agony, and he has learned to live with it. He can easily get a prescription for pain-killing drugs, but he refuses. Don says it shuts down his other systems. One time he said, "It makes me feel like a zombie." Occasionally at night the pain gets extremely bad, and he takes something for relief, but that's the exception rather than a daily routine.

I don't want to lose Don, and I believe we still have good years left together; however, I know that when he does leave, he'll go to a place where he can jump and run and do all the things he can't do now. Although sad for myself, I'll be happy for him.

Don made me promise that if he's ever hit by a truck again or involved in one of those life-threatening situations, I'll not pray for him to recover.

I understand that now, and I've promised. When he does pass from this life, there will be joy in the fact that I'll know he's without that every-minute-of-the-day pain in his body. Even now, I ache when I realize how much he hurts. I believe I could handle my own pain better than to watch the way it hurts him.

33.
MOVING ON

We often say that when God calls a person to be a pastor, he calls the whole family. That's certainly been true for us. From the time Don felt God wanted him to be a pastor, I felt led to be a pastor's wife and was convinced it was my calling, along with being a teacher. Through our marriage Don has supported my career; I've supported his.

Being part of a minister's family means being open to God's call to move. In the summer of 1990, we followed his call when Don accepted the position of pastor at the First Baptist Church in Rosharon, Texas. It was the first church where he was the senior pastor. I had some adjusting to do in my new role as the pastor's wife. Rosharon wasn't a big church. The attendance was anywhere from seventy-five to a hundred people on Sunday morning. I was younger than most of the women in the congregation, which was a new experience for me because we'd previously been at churches with a wide variety of ages.

Rosharon was a fine experience for Don. I observed his growth, especially in the way he cared for others. He learned to delegate responsibility, which I hadn't seen him do before.

I also grew during that time. I had good relationships at Rosharon,

but I had to learn the boundary lines and protect myself by not saying too much or expressing my opinion too often. I wasn't protecting
only myself but my family as well. I found that whenever I spoke, it
was taken as a voice of authority—even though I didn't feel that way.

As the pastor's wife, I didn't want to appear to be taking sides on
church issues. If asked, I would share my thoughts, but in a way that
was not confrontational. The confidence I had gained during Don's
hospital stay served me well in presenting my ideas.

At Rosharon we lived in the parsonage out in the middle of a rice
field. That was difficult for me because I grew up a city girl, even
with all my dad's military transfers. We were usually housed on an
Air Force base. For the first time in my life, I was living in a rural
area with snakes and mosquitoes. However, our boys, who were then
nine, still say it was the best place they ever lived. They went into the
fields, captured snakes, and brought them back to the house. They
had unlimited space for playing. I loved the people and the church,
but I wasn't happy living where we were. As much as I enjoyed the
people, and I truly did, I didn't enjoy country life.

We stayed at Rosharon nearly three years, and they were three
good years. Afterward, with God's direction, Don resigned from the
church to move to Plano, Texas. He had heard about an opening at a
Christian radio station in the Dallas area. Radio and TV have always
attracted him. Another factor was that David Gentiles had become
the youth pastor of Hunter's Glen Baptist Church in Plano. Because
David was his best friend, I think Don wanted to be close to him. I
was excited to be back in the city.

On the downside, moving meant I had to give up my teaching
position in Alvin. We moved to Plano even though I had no job.

Don was employed by the radio station, but like many Christian-
service organizations, they didn't pay well. I needed a job, and we also
needed the insurance.

One night after church, a new friend who worked for Plano
Independent School District told me she had arranged a meeting

for me to interview for a teaching position at a new school. There were no first-grade positions open, but the school needed a third-grade teacher who would work with gifted-level students. I took the position. Once again, I was out of my comfort zone; but to my amazement, I enjoyed teaching those gifted children.

In 1994, I was elected and honored to be named teacher of the year at Mitchell Elementary. That truly was a big deal for me. The change from teaching first grade to teaching third allowed some of my unused talents to mature. Accepting the third-grade position was another one of God's hidden blessings.

During that time Don continued working for the radio station, but he wasn't finding a lot of meaning in his life. He went to work, and he was successful, but it was obvious he wasn't happy. He didn't feel fulfilled.

One day he told me, "I've decided to resign." He added, "I don't have anywhere else to go, but it's time for me to leave."

"You're going to do *what*?"

"I'll find something."

He was calmer about his decision than I was. But I knew Don had prayed about that decision, and he believed it was the right thing to do.

"I know it will work out for you—for us." I was able to say that honestly and sincerely.

God came through for him. On the outskirts of Plano is a small town called Murphy. Almost as soon as he resigned, Don accepted a call to pastor Murphy Road Baptist Church. It was a little larger than Rosharon, with perhaps 100 to 150 people on Sunday.

Don enjoyed being there. I could see the difference in his attitude. He became more upbeat and assured.

I developed several fine friends there, and I was ready to stay until retirement. But God had different plans. We stayed a couple of years, and at the end of 1996, we moved to Pasadena, a suburb of Houston.

Our legal agreement was that as long as Dr. Greider was able to see Don, that's where we had to go. It wasn't such a big deal in itself,

but we didn't know how often Don would need serious medical attention. The more we prayed about it, the more certain Don felt that we
needed to move back into the Houston area.

Don accepted the call to serve as single-adult minister at First
Baptist Church, Pasadena. Our entire family was actively involved in
various areas of the church. The congregation was warm and friendly.
We easily made friends and began to build those relationships.

A church member worked to get me a job with the Deer Park
Independent School District. My heart soared when I discovered they
needed a third-grade teacher. I was sure this was where we would
spend the rest of our lives.

But God had yet another plan.

34.

TIME FOR A BOOK

In January of 2002, Don started having serious health problems, such as heart palpitations and difficulty breathing. "I feel like an elephant is sitting on my chest."

He had one of those spells at church on a Sunday morning. Several members were medical personnel, and they carried pagers so they could rush to any emergency for first aid or whatever was needed.

Don went into the library and was very pale. "I feel awful," he said.

Someone called a nurse named Sue Mulholland. She took his blood pressure, and it was extremely high. "We need to get you to the emergency room."

She called me out of the congregation, and I drove him to St. John's Hospital, where he was admitted. A doctor listened to Don's heart and kept him for two days to run tests. Nothing showed up—not a thing.

When they rushed Don to the hospital, my first thought was, *Here we go again*. I didn't know what was going on. I wasn't sure if I ought to go to school the next day. Many of those old fears came rushing back. Once again I strongly felt I had to be in the hospital with him, as if my being there could protect him. When I visited him

Sunday afternoon, I said I'd take a personal day and spend Monday at the hospital.

"No, don't," Don said. "I'm fine. Go ahead and work."

He persuaded me to go to school Monday, but as soon as my classes were over, I rushed to the hospital. During the day I called to check on him whenever I could break away from my students. The possibility of losing him was very real because I'd walked that fearsome road before.

Staff were still running tests, but they couldn't find anything wrong. They ran a few more tests, with the same results, so they dismissed him.

The symptoms continued, not each day, but every now and then. Don would feel light-headed, hear ringing in his ears, and become short of breath. We went to other doctors, including cardiologists and respiratory therapists. It seemed as though each contradicted what the previous doctor had said. None of them found the cause. My frustration and anxiety were growing as Don's symptoms continued.

Finally, one of the nurses at our church recommended a doctor at the Houston Medical Center. "If he can't find out what's wrong with you, nobody can."

We made an appointment, and Don went alone because I was unable to leave school. He and the doctor talked through everything. In the course of their conversation, Don mentioned that he was writing the book about his accident.

That was what the doctor needed to hear. He said, "You're suffering from PTSS—post traumatic stress syndrome. You're reliving everything that happened to you while you're writing the book."

"That makes sense to me," Don said with relief. At last he had a diagnosis. "Should I stop?"

"No, you need to finish the book. Only then can you move on with the next part of your life."

When I heard the PTSS diagnosis, I felt a profound sense of relief. "This is something we can deal with. We can handle this."

I had long encouraged Don to write about his experience because I felt it was a story that needed to be told. Now I was a little more adamant.

Several times I asked, "How's the book coming?" because for me the real message was, "We need to move on and get it written." I had to fight to keep the take-charge, recovery-created part of my personality in control.

I felt we needed to make that next step—to close that chapter on our life. To do that, Don needed to write the book. I didn't know if it would be published, but that wasn't as much a concern for me as it was to have him finish writing it.

My biggest fear was that people might make fun of Don or question whether the story was true. That came from the protective side of me. Yet, I felt he needed to write the book to move on with his life. I also believed it was an important story that needed to be shared.

Don did complete the manuscript.

In 2003, Don went to a writers' conference, where author Cecil Murphey (Cec) was teaching. Don was impressed with him and asked him to write his story. To his credit, Cec said he'd pray about helping Don with the book. After further discussion with Don, he agreed to write the story. Together they wrote the book, and a publisher bought it.

———

One afternoon Don came home with a FedEx envelope and sat down. "Come here," he said. "I want to show you something." As soon as I sat down, he pulled out his first copy of the book, *90 Minutes in Heaven*.

I was so proud of him for getting that project done. It was delightful to see the entire book in manuscript form, and to see the actual book was amazing. It's almost like looking at a new baby—I wanted to touch it, smell it, and keep looking.

We didn't talk a lot about the book, but I was proud of him, and I knew he was overjoyed.

We both assumed we'd sell a few copies to church members. Our parents would want a copy. I'd heard about people who had their garages full of unsold books, and I'd even been to their homes. Typically, sometime before we left, the writer in the family would say, "Hey, I've written a book . . ." He would then either try to sell it to us or, more often, give us a free copy.

That was what we expected for Don's book.

God surprised us.

In fall of 2004, *90 Minutes in Heaven* was released. Almost immediately, Don received offers from churches and organizations to speak about his experience. I assumed it would last a few weeks, but it didn't let up. More and more opportunities came.

A short time after the book came out, Don felt it was time to move again. A church in south Houston was without a pastor, and they contacted Don. He sent them his résumé and talked with the committee. Then Don visited the facilities, and it looked as if that would be his next move.

But God intervened.

Don flew to Atlanta, where he had been invited to speak about his experience. While he was gone, I fielded thirty phone calls from churches, and all of them wanted Don to preach. Every caller had read *90 Minutes in Heaven*. "We believe he has an important message we need to hear."

It was late in the week by the time the calls came in, and that Sunday we were supposed to be at the church in south Houston to preach "in view of a call."

Don called me to let me know how things were going in Atlanta. When he asked how things were in Pasadena, I said, laughing, "I feel like I'm a receptionist for you."

"What do you mean?" He had no idea of the responses to the book.

"I've received thirty telephone calls for you." I had written down the information and kept count. "All of them want you to come to their church and preach."

In the meantime, the committee at the church in south Houston was waiting for Don to give them an answer so they could present his name after he preached.

Don paused for a moment, then asked, "What do you think? Should we say yes to the church?"

"I've prayed and prayed about this, and I don't feel that's what you need to do right now."

"Why not?"

"Right now, I don't think you need to become a pastor. I don't think you should accept this call."

"What am I going to do? We have kids and bills and—"

"I think that right now your ministry is *90 Minutes in Heaven*."

"That would be a gigantic leap of faith, because we have no idea what kind of income that will generate." The logical side of Don had come out again.

"There are no benefits associated with publishing," he continued. "We don't know if these offers are going to keep coming. They're tumbling in right now, but who knows how long that's going to be."

"I realize that," I said, "but I think you need to go on the road and speak as often as you're asked."

"I want to pastor a church," he said softly. "You know that."

I was bold in my response. "If God wants you to be the pastor of a church, he will give you a church when it's time for you to have one. Until then I feel this is what you need to do."

After we talked a little more, he said, "I'll call the chairman of the pulpit committee tonight and write them a letter. Then I need to promote the book," he continued, "and speak as often as I'm asked. I'll do it for six months and see what happens."

I smiled. I was delighted to have him repeat my words back to me.

Neither of us had any idea what it would mean for Don to take such a drastic step. I'm writing this nearly ten years later. He's still getting calls and sets up most of his speaking a year in advance.

35.

LINGERING EFFECTS

Even now, Don still deals with depression occasionally, although it's not severe the way it was in the hospital. We don't know whether it's a residual side effect from the accident or if it's that yearning to leave this world and go back to his permanent home in heaven.

When the depression hits him, it's usually after he's been on the road for a long time and he's worn out. He maintains a speaking schedule that exceeds that of most public speakers. Don's aware of his limited time on earth, certainly in ways I don't comprehend. He's committed to the words of Jesus and following his example: "The night is coming, and then no one can work" (John 9:4).

His depression is worse at some times than at others. I know my husband well enough that I can sense when it's coming back. Another factor for the recurring depression may be that Don refuses to stay heavily medicated for the pain. So part of his gloominess may be the pain sneaking through his consciousness.

Don is a kind man, and I know that. I also know that when he's depressed, he slips back into the frame of mind where he won't talk to me. Just like before, at times I feel left out and lonely. He doesn't set out to be hurtful, but it's the depression troubling him.

Now that I understand depression better, I've learned to walk out of the room when he's feeling his worst. I know that given some time alone to rest and regroup, he will come out of the depressive state more quickly. I have to accept the fact that I can't fix everything for him, but he knows I'm there to talk when he decides to open up.

Most of the time I'm strong enough to deal with his gloominess. I also admit that at times I don't handle it well, especially if there are other things going on in our lives.

For instance, I retired from teaching in 2009. Before that, however, if I had a bad day at school and had to come home and face his sense of despair, at times I lashed out at Don. That's something I never thought I'd do. But it happens, and both of us always feel bad about it afterward.

I understand some of what he's going through, although I'm not sure the kids do. They know their dad went through a horrific accident and the torturous battle afterward, but I'm not convinced they truly grasp how much pain he still suffers on a day-to-day basis, because he looks healthy. Our children are now grown, but when we're around and they see Don in his low moods, they're protective of me. They sometimes become angry or frustrated with him.

"You always come to his defense," they say.

And I do.

They love their father, but they don't get the full picture regarding his suffering—and I don't blame them for it. Nicole was older, and she understands a little more than the boys. She has more pre-wreck memories to draw from. A few times, however, she's been exasperated and said, "That's Dad. And he can be difficult."

Don isn't unkind because he wants to be. It's just that when he's on the road for a lengthy period, speaking perhaps fifteen times in two weeks, he comes home exhausted. That's when the depression seems worse.

I've been present when Don has ministered to people as he signed books. Repeatedly he hears stories of grief, tragedy, and despair. He listens and offers comforting words, but the sum total of those heartaches is overwhelming. He knows there are more needs than he can ever attend to.

That's also when he's apt to snap at me. I understand that's not the real Don who's irritated, so I've learned not to take it personally. I love him, and because I do, I tell him that he can be a grouchy old man around me as much as he needs to be. It brings a laugh, and things actually get a little better.

I also admire Don since he covers his continued physical problems well. He can't do some simple things, like get down on his knees. That's still difficult because he used to play ball with the boys without falling down. Now just getting out of a chair can be difficult.

———

In the fifteen years we were married before the accident, Don didn't go through bouts of depression. As for any normal human being, there were times of discouragement and letdown. That's different from the change that came over him in the hospital. Because I hadn't previously observed that kind of behavior, it's clear to me that his depression is a direct or indirect result of the accident. Regardless of the cause, he had a distinct change in his personality and became different in many ways.

That's the negative. On the positive side, he has learned to appreciate his family more. He wants them around him as much as possible. The occasional conflict we face is that Don sometimes, on his own, plans something for the family. The conflict happens because he fails to tell us, and we have made other commitments. He is adamant that he did tell us. We jokingly say, "Must be the short-term memory loss from the wreck."

We laugh. And we find ways to work things out.

Don was always serious and zealous to serve Jesus Christ, but he's more so now. Despite his physical limitations, he gives of himself and holds nothing in reserve. There are times I wish he would slow down and take better care of himself. Yet when I watch him speak and hear the passion in his voice as he tells about heaven, I know he can't rest. I'm proud of him. He does more than most healthy men. I consider myself lucky to be married to such a strong, determined man.

I believe those who suffer from trauma and tragedy, along with those who love them, are changed in some way for the rest of their lives. It's like taking a piece of paper and tearing it in half. We can tape it back together, write on it, draw a picture, or cover it in lipstick kisses, but the tear will always be there.

The paper is still useful, but it can't be as it was before. That's not an overall bad thing. If we think about it, the place where it is taped is the strongest part of the page.

Don is different; I'm different; our kids are different, but we are stronger in many ways.

That's God's grace.

36.
WHERE WE ARE

After Don made his decision not to accept the call to be a pastor again, things took off quickly. Seemingly, the phone rang nonstop. He resigned from his position at First Baptist Church of Pasadena, and I kept teaching at Deer Park Elementary School.

When Don wasn't on the road, he'd be home, so we set up a home office for him. Oddly enough, at first I felt as if he were encroaching on my space, although both of us adjusted.

There was an excitement about this new life, and Don enjoyed living it. He didn't say it, but I think that's when Don began to grasp why God had sent him back to earth.

———

Shortly after we married, Don often talked about being an evangelist. He said he wanted to give people the gospel and point them to Jesus Christ. After the book sales took off and doors kept opening in the United States and all over the world, I thought, *You know what? God answered that prayer—not exactly as Don had planned, but it's a definite answer.*

God does that sometimes. We may not get what we ask for right then, but he has something even better down the road. God blessed our willingness to step out in faith. The best part of this new life is that through Don Piper Ministries, based on *90 Minutes in Heaven*, he is able to minister to people all over the world—whether in person or through his other books.

I think back to the fact that he wanted to minister to that congregation in south Houston because he truly cares about people. God has given him an even bigger "congregation." Instead of a few hundred people, he can reach thousands. As his wife, I'm proud of his decision, and I know he did the right thing.

"I survived, and Eva overcame." Many times I've listened to Don make that statement from the pulpit. He goes on to say, "Eva is the heroine of my story."

I don't feel much like a heroine; I feel like an ordinary elementary school teacher who did what needed to be done. When people come to the book table and say to me, "I want to shake your hand," or "I want to hug you and tell you what a wonderful woman you must be," it humbles me because I don't feel I deserve special recognition.

I did walk in the dark—for a long time—but I also believe that almost any Christian woman would do what I did. I could have done better, but being a caregiver is almost always on-the-job training. I learned as I went along. I accepted the fact that I would never do a perfect job, and I didn't do everything right. But I kept trying.

If we stay connected to God and are open to receive good advice from our family and friends and pray for wisdom, we'll do all right. Most of the time, we'll make the right decisions.

I also learned not to look back and tell myself what I might have done or how I could have done it better. It was the best I knew to do at the time, and that's usually good enough. I learned to make decisions and stick with them.

Sometimes my ideas and decisions didn't work well, and I learned to accept myself for being human. I didn't have to be the super-achieving wife; I had to be only Eva Piper—the best possible Eva Piper I could become.

37.

BECAUSE

At the end of my husband's book *90 Minutes in Heaven*, he wrote a chapter of "why" questions. By now we have answers to some of those questions. Some answers have changed through the years.

When I was finally convinced to write my story, my goal was to provide meaningful information to those in a caregiving role. I often tell people, "I don't have all the answers, but I made it through a dark time. Along the way I gained much insight into how to survive."

I also strongly feel each person needs to be prepared for whatever circumstances life throws at you. I certainly didn't wake up on the morning of January 18, 1989, thinking, *Today I will start being a caregiver.* As a Girl Scout, I learned the motto Be Prepared. That is a good motto for life because, for most people, it's not *if* they or someone they love will deal with some type of traumatic circumstance, but *when*. In response to the "whys," here are some "becauses."

Because crises and tragedies are unexpected, you need to have a plan. Don't wait to discuss your thoughts about a living will, end-of-life care, and funeral plans. Those aren't pleasant conversations, but for the loved one having to make life-and-death decisions, it is a blessing not to have to say, "I wonder what he [or she] would want."

Each responsible adult should know where important papers, such as insurance policies, bank statements, deeds, and medical records are kept. Keeping important papers in a marked file will help the caregiver access information.

While most families divide the responsibilities, everyone needs to have a working knowledge of how the family runs with regard to finances and household maintenance. The less a caregiver has to learn while providing for his or her loved one, the more energy is available for that loved one's care.

Because you'll need a great deal of support, develop healthy relationships with your family and friends. This may sound simplistic, but in today's busy world, too many of us are engaged in surface relationships.

Relationships take time, and they require effort. A great place to start is becoming part of a church family. Our church family ministered to us in innumerable ways because they loved and cared for us.

The main purpose of the church is to minister to those in need. Being part of a church allows you the chance to minister to others and to benefit from their care when your need arises.

Both family and friend relationships are made stronger by being there for the good and happy times as well as the trying and difficult ones. That may mean not watching a favorite TV show or missing an event to spend quality time with the important people in your life.

At times relationships require sacrifice, but the rewards are amazing. Look for ways to reach out to help. Keep the lines of communication open. It's easy to hide what's really going on in our lives behind e-mails and social networking. You need face-to-face communication or at least to hear a voice on the phone. That helps you get a better picture of how your family and friends are doing and vice versa. Without my family and friends I could never have found my way along that dark path following Don's accident.

Because we are God's children, we must also strengthen our relationships with him. One of the best ways to do that is through prayer. Prayer is more than a list of wants and thank-yous, although they are important. To build your prayer life, you need to learn to talk openly and honestly with God throughout your day.

There's no required length to a prayer; it may be just a sentence or two. At other times you may find yourself spending significant time talking to and listening to God. As you practice turning over the little things in your life to God through prayer, it becomes easier and more natural to turn to him in the crises of life.

God always hears the prayers of his children, but it's so much easier to pray during those difficult times when you've had lots of practice. Don't wait until the crisis hits to call out to God. Instead, make it a part of your day-to-day living.

Because God loves you, you need to spend time building up your faith and trust in him. Proverbs 3:5–6, verses many of us learned as children, reads, "Trust in the LORD with all your heart; do not depend on your own understanding. Seek his will in all you do, and he will show you which path to take." I didn't really understand what that meant until Don's accident. If you think about the word *depend* (or *lean*, in some translations), it means your own understanding isn't enough to support or hold you up. I've been guilty of saying I trust God, but then taking things into my own hands.

Too often I depend on my understanding of how to handle a problem. I like to be in control. After Don's accident I had no control, and so there was no choice except to turn it over to God. I'm still learning to exercise my "trust muscles." By trusting God with the smaller things in my life, I build up and strengthen those muscles. Then, when something heavy comes into my life, it's easier to turn the problem over to him. While I may not always understand God's plan, I know it's the perfect plan for my life.

I also build my faith by reading and studying God's Word. There are so many promises and lessons throughout the Bible. They bless and calm my heart each time I read them. It may be an ancient book, but it shines a light on my life every time I read it. "Your word is a lamp to guide my feet and a light for my path" (Ps. 119:105). God's Word shone a light on my dark path and still guides me today.

38.

WHEN THE DARKNESS
COMES AGAIN

It took a while, but eventually I came out of the dark. There were
many heartaches, trials, and hurts, but also strengthened friendships, a renewed prayer life, and a closer walk with my Lord. There
are those who think once you've overcome a tragedy, you never have
to face heartache again. Sad to say, I have had more experiences of
walking in the dark.

The phone rang as I was trying to get everyone ready to head to
church for Wednesday night activities on April 12, 2000. Looking at
the caller ID, I recognized my parents' home number, so I grabbed the
phone and said hello, expecting to hear the words, "I just needed to
hear my number one daughter's voice." Instead, my dad explained that
my sister-in-law, Joyce Pentecost, had just been diagnosed with stage
4 melanoma.

I was in shock. I felt the darkness closing in on me again.

Joyce was a vivacious redhead with an incredible voice. Earlier
that year she had cut her first CD of Christian hymns and gospel
songs. She and Eddie had just made the decision to go into full-time

Christian ministry. They planned to travel, along with their two young children, to various revivals and retreats, where Joyce would provide the special music.

Now Dad was telling me Joyce and Eddie would be coming to Houston to meet with doctors at MD Anderson Cancer Center, so of course they would stay with us and travel to the hospital for more tests. Over the next year Joyce fought bravely to overcome the cancer that had invaded her brain, lungs, and abdomen. At first she seemed to be winning the fight.

Our family prayed, our churches prayed, and our friends prayed for complete healing. I envisioned Joyce and Don being on the same stage, talking about their miracles of survival. I couldn't believe God would take a young wife and mother. I was wrong.

On May 3, 2001, once again my phone rang. "She's gone," Dad said.

That year I walked in the dark alongside my brother. Often we talked about Don's accident and recovery. Because I had experienced the ups and downs of Don's recovery, I could relate to his frustration and anxiety. I understood when he wanted to talk as well as when he needed to recharge.

Along with many others, we made our way down the dark path and back into the light. My dark walk after Don's accident helped me provide extra light for Eddie.

The darkness wasn't over.

Don and I were headed to the airport on October 19, 2009. We were both scheduled to speak at the WinSome Women's Conference on Macinaw Island, Michigan. My cell phone rang, and I saw my brother's name. I answered, knowing Don and I needed to leave.

"Mom's had a stroke," my brother said. "She's in the hospital, and it looks pretty bad."

The darkness descended.

I told him I was canceling my speaking engagement and heading home.

"No, Dad said to tell you that he and Mom want you to go ahead.

You've made a commitment and need to keep it. I'll call if there are any changes."

Reluctantly I agreed. During the three-day conference more than three thousand women prayed for my mother. Their care and concern for someone they had never met were powerful. So many women reached out to me to offer comfort.

After we returned to Houston, we drove to my parents' home. Over the next three and a half months, I traveled the road between Houston and Shreveport multiple times. Most weeks I spent three to four days sitting with my mom in the hospital and then drove back to Houston.

In many ways I was reliving my experience with Don. Dad stayed each night at the hospital with her. He refused to sleep away from her. My being there meant he could go home to shower, take a nap, or run errands. My mom had lost her speech, so someone needed to be with her around the clock.

Once again I saw the arms of Jesus reach out to help my dad. Friends from his church, some of whom I had known since high school, brought food, mowed the yard, or sat with Mom if Dad and I both needed to be away. Little by little Mom improved. She couldn't speak, but her physical therapy was helping her regain some movement on her right side.

I decided that we would go ahead with our planned family vacation to Disney World. After caring for my mom, I needed a break, and Dad encouraged me to go. The entire family, including our granddaughter, headed to Orlando. Don was tired after speaking earlier that week, but by the second day he had rested and was ready to head out to dinner.

Just then, Chris knocked on our door and asked, "Dad, have you talked to Cliff? He needs you to call him right away. David Gentiles has been in an accident."

My little bit of light from taking a break was extinguished immediately.

During the next few hours, we were told David had suffered an accident while lifting weights at a gym. The prognosis wasn't good.

My darkness was getting murkier and murkier.

Don and Chris flew out the following morning to be at David's bedside. When Don called that night, I knew the news wasn't good. David was on life support; there was no brain activity. They were waiting for one of his daughters, who was traveling abroad, to arrive before disconnecting the machines.

David died on December 18, 2009.

Again I cried out to God. "Why? Why would you take someone as kind and good-hearted as David, a minister who has given up everything to serve you?" As always, God sent a peace to me. There was no answer, but the complete peace of knowing God is in control soothed my heart.

———

A little more than a month later, on January 27, 2010, my mom died after getting an infection from having catheters, IVs, and a feeding tube. Her body wasn't strong enough to fight any longer.

I sat with my dad and my brother, watching Mom take her final breaths. After her last breath, we stood with our arms around each other. I thought about our lives—my losing, then regaining my husband; Eddie losing his young wife; the loss of our dear friend David Gentiles; and Dad losing his wife of fifty-nine years. We could have been angry, bitter, and lost, but instead there was a peace in the room.

We had all walked in the dark but had emerged on the other side with the help of family, friends, prayer, and faith.

The darkness isn't over. We face it at the most unexpected times. But we can be prepared. God has never left us to walk through the dark alone, and he won't leave you either.

All praise to God, the Father of our Lord Jesus Christ. God is our merciful Father and the source of all comfort. He comforts us in all our troubles so that we can comfort others. When they are troubled, we will be able to give them the same comfort God has given us.

—2 Corinthians 1:3–4

ACKNOWLEDGMENTS

T here is a saying that every person has a book inside of him or her. You are holding mine. For me, that's an amazing statement. There have been times in my life when I toyed with the idea of writing a career book, a book about my family, or even a children's book, but never a crisis book. After hearing the same question repeatedly, "When are you going to write a book?" it became evident this was a book people not only wanted but felt was needed— a book that honestly talks about how to survive and move ahead when tragedy strikes. To place this book in your hands took the support and help of many people.

I first met my coauthor, Cecil Murphey, when he came to our home to work with my husband on the book *90 Minutes in Heaven* in 2003. As the years have passed, Cec has become a dear friend of our family. His patience with me, along with his massive doses of encouragement, has meant more than I can say. Thank you, Cec. You are a blessing.

My agent, Deidre Knight, of the Knight Agency, is another person who came into our lives through *90 Minutes in Heaven*. Never in my wildest dreams would I have imagined when Don and I met her to eat at Pappasito's Mexican Restaurant in Houston that one day she would be working with me to get my own book published. She is an amazing woman, and I'm honored to call her my friend.

I believe one of God's greatest blessings is Christian friends. Throughout my life I've had the honor and privilege to have many. I'm glad for this opportunity to thank two friends who go far beyond being special, Ginny Wagner and Carla Cothran. Both have had their own walks in the dark and emerged into the light. Their suggestions, care, support, and listening ears while I wrote this book have sustained me on so many levels. You are two of God's greatest blessings in my life. I love you, Ginny and Carla.

How do you adequately thank the people who gave you life? My parents, Eldon and Ethel Pentecost, raised me with love. That love was demonstrated over and over as I tried to make it through those dark days following Don's accident. There are no words big enough, strong enough, or beautiful enough to express my thanks. Mom and Dad, your sacrifice of time and energy meant I could focus on caring for Don. You were always there to listen and most important, to pray. I love you, Daddy, and I miss you, Mama. Thank you for having such a big part in making me who I am.

Two of the happiest days in my life were the births of our daughter, Nicole, and our twin boys, Chris and Joe. As your mother, I'm proud of the adults you have become. Each of you has unique and special talents that you use to honor your Lord. No mother could ask for more. During my dark days you brightened my walk each time I was able to see you or talk to you. Just thinking about you makes my day go better. I love you Nicole, my favorite daughter; Chris, my favorite brown-headed son; and Joe, my favorite redheaded son.

Without my husband's love and support, this book would never have happened. Don has always had more faith in my abilities than I have had in myself. Don travels all over the world, but I can always count on the phone ringing each night at ten o'clock, just so he can check in and see how I am. During the past thirty-nine years of marriage, we've walked many roads, some bright, some dark, but you've never left my side. Thank you for your belief in me, thank you for loving our incredible children, thank you for being an indulging papa to our grandchildren, and thank you for being a man who seeks to do God's will. You are my hero.

It would take pages and pages to thank all the people who have been there and supported Don and me in our ministry through the years. The people at South Park Baptist Church, First Baptist–Rosharon, Murphy Road Baptist, and First Baptist–Pasadena have been encouraging, loving, and supportive. My life is so much fuller having known you and been loved by you.

I want to thank all the teachers with whom I've worked, especially the first-grade team at Stevenson Primary, who stood in the gap for me. I can never forget your kindness and your willingness to take up the slack. It touched my heart. You were truly my life support, and I continue to thank God for you.

Thank you, Lord. I owe everything to your love and care. When I answer the question, "How did you do it?" I say simply, "With God." I mean it from the depths of my heart and soul. Thank you, Jesus, for being with me every step of the way, even when at times I didn't recognize your presence. You light my life with faith and hope for better tomorrows. My heart is yours.

Eva L. Piper

ABOUT THE AUTHOR

Eva Piper is a speaker and author with a unique insight into the trials of heartache and the triumph of overcoming. She has inspired audiences with her testimony of walking her hurting loved ones through a dark night and surviving to see a sunrise not just bright but much more beautiful because of the journey. The wife of best-selling author Don Piper, Eva was the glue that held her broken husband and her family together.

Don's story, recounted in the *New York Times* bestseller *90 Minutes in Heaven: A True Story of Life and Death*, is Eva's story too. In fact, today Don calls her the "real hero" of their ordeal.

She and Don now live in Pasadena, Texas. She is a cum laude graduate of Louisiana State University. A teacher for thirty-four years, she received Teacher of the Year honors in the Plano, Texas, Independent School District, served as an adjunct professor at North Texas State University, and guest lecturer for the Education Service Center.

About the Writer

Cecil Murphey is the author or coauthor of more than a hundred books, including *Making Sense When Life Doesn't*. He has written four books with Don Piper, beginning with *90 Minutes in Heaven*. *Gifted Hands*, written for Dr. Ben Carson, has remained a big seller since publication in 1990 and is now in its seventy-third printing.

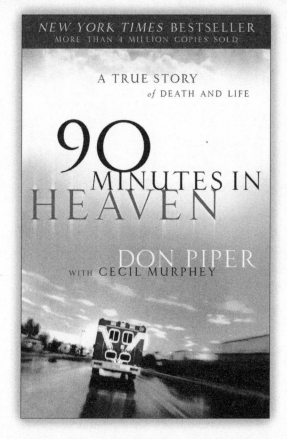